Unseen Unheard Unknown

Sarah Hamilton-Byrne was adopted at birth and, unbeknown to her natural mother, she was quickly passed on to Anne Hamilton-Byrne, the leader of the secret cult that called itself The Family. Sarah and other falsely acquired children were brought up in extreme isolation on one of The Family's properties at Lake Eildon, Victoria. In 1987 police rescued the children in a dramatic early-morning raid. Sarah and the freed children spent the next years in care, first at Allambie and then at the St John's Homes for Boys and Girls.

Since 1987 Sarah has been one of the most outspoken critics of Anne Hamilton-Byrne's beliefs, influence and methods of recruiting and retaining members of The Family. Despite the difficulties of learning to live in the outside world and of coping with constant media attention and numerous court cases, Sarah managed to complete her secondary education and a degree in Medicine at the University of Melbourne. Towards the end of her time at university, she gained medical experience in Thailand and India. Since graduating as a doctor, Sarah Hamilton-Byrne has practised in Victorian hospitals.

UNSEEN
UNHEARD
UNKNOWN

Sarah Hamilton-Byrne

Penguin Books

Penguin Books Australia Ltd
487 Maroondah Highway, PO Box 257
Ringwood, Victoria 3134, Australia
Penguin Books Ltd
Harmondsworth, Middlesex, England
Viking Penguin, A Division of Penguin Books USA Inc.
375 Hudson Street, New York, New York 10014, USA
Penguin Books Canada Limited
10 Alcorn Avenue, Toronto, Ontario, Canada M4V 3B2
Penguin Books (N.Z.) Ltd
182–190 Wairau Road, Auckland 10, New Zealand

First published by Penguin Books Australia Ltd 1995

1 3 5 7 9 10 8 6 4 2

Copyright © Sarah Hamilton-Byrne, 1995

All rights reserved. Without limiting the rights under copyright reserved above, no part of this publication may be reproduced, stored in or introduced into a retrieval system, or transmitted, in any form or by any means (electronic, mechanical, photocopying, recording or otherwise), without the prior written permission of both the copyright owner and the above publisher of this book.

Typeset in Sabon by Midland Typesetters, Maryborough, Victoria
Front cover photograph of the author by Heather Dinas
Printed in Australia by Australian Print Group, Maryborough, Victoria

National Library of Australia
Cataloguing-in-Publication data

Hamilton-Byrne, Sarah, 1969 – .
Unseen unheard unknown: my life inside The Family of
Anne Hamilton-Byrne.

ISBN 0 14 017434 6.

1. Hamilton-Byrne, Sarah 2. Hamilton-Byrne, Anne.
3. Ex-cultists – Biography. 4. Cults – Australia.
I. Title.

305.62899

Contents

Dedication – vii

Prologue – 1

1
Early on – 6

2
A day in my life – 17

3
My aunties – 38

4
Suffer the little children – 46

5
The hungry years – 65

6
All creatures great and small – 81

7
Outsiders – 88

8
My mother, my master – 99

9
The world according to Anne – 115

10
Initiation into The Family – 130

11
Going-through – 139

12
'Go and die in the gutter' – 151

13
The raid – 167

14
Aftermath – 179

15
Answers to old questions – 194

16
My journey to survival – 204

Dedication

This account is dedicated to the brothers and sisters I grew up with and still love with all my heart; to Ed, who first convinced me that life was worth living and believed that I could make it; to Denise and Sue, who demonstrated to me what unconditional love and affection meant; to Erica and her family for taking me into their home when I was most needy; to Marie for her support, courage and determination to seek justice for us; to my mother, Mal and my baby sisters, who are showing me what being in a loving family means at last.

This book is also dedicated to Baba Muktananda, who showed me as a small child what a true spiritual guru was like: I thank him for being there to follow and believe in at a crucial time in my life.

As well, I thank the many others whose support and belief in me helped me in my journey to survival: Ola, Mick, Helen D., Doctor David H., Hans and Krissy, and my lovers, Steve and John. Thanks also to Deb for helping me write this book and for her friendship.

Prologue

My name is Sarah Hamilton-Byrne. I am one of the children of The Family and this is the story of my childhood spent in that cult.

The woman who I grew up believing was my mother was Anne Hamilton-Byrne, the leader of The Family or the Great White Brotherhood, a small cult in the Dandenongs. I was a small part of Anne Hamilton-Byrne's plan to collect children in what she called a 'scientific experiment'. Later I discovered it was her intention that we children would continue her cult after the earth was consumed by a holocaust. She saw us as the 'inheritors of the earth'. I didn't know that then. In those days I was just a child. A child of a guru, but a child none the less.

I often wonder just what it was Anne wanted of us, what need drove her to collect all of us children and to make this false 'family'. Was it just to satisfy her ego? To satisfy her great need to be worshipped and adored by those around her?

Why did Anne raise us in almost total social isolation, kilometres from anywhere and with minimal contact with other humans apart from the cult members who looked after us? Why did she subject us to the bizarre and cruel regimen in which we grew up? Was it to demonstrate that she had the power to create a generation reared in her beliefs and believing her to be the

Master? I suspect that there were more sinister motives than these alone. Of the fourteen or so children who carried her name, some had multiple birth certificates and passports, and citizenship of more than one country. Only she knows why this was and why we were all dressed alike; why most of us had our hair dyed blond. I can only conjecture because I will never know for sure. However, I suspect that she went to such great lengths in order to move children around, in and out of the country. Perhaps even to be sold overseas. I'm sure there is a market somewhere in the world for small blond children with no traceable identities. If she did it, it was a perfect scam. Many ex-cult members have said that they were aware that Anne was creating children by a 'breeding programme' in the late 1960s. These were 'invisible' kids because they had no papers, and there is no proof that they ever existed. We Hamilton-Byrne children had multiple identities so perhaps these were loaned to other children and the similarity of our appearance used to cover up the absence of these children. One small blond kid looks very like another in a passport photo. I don't suppose we will ever know for sure because only Anne Hamilton-Byrne knows the truth about the whole affair, and the truth is something she will never tell.

In 1987 my life in the cult came to an end. The police raided the Eildon property on which we children had grown up, and we were taken into the protective custody of Community Services Victoria (CSV). A number of charges were laid and about seven of the cult members who had been our minders were convicted of social security fraud. In 1989 a police taskforce was set up to investigate the alleged activities of Anne and her husband, Bill, who had left the country, and in mid-1993 they were extradited to Australia from the United States to face only one charge: that of conspiracy to commit perjury in relation to the false registration of some of us children. The Hamilton-Byrnes fought this charge through the courts for eighteen months, taking it right up to the Full Bench of the Supreme Court, hiring the best Queen's Counsel who were experts on international law. Eventually the charge was overturned on the basis that there was no jurisdiction within Victorian law to prosecute something that effectively took place in New Zealand. The terms of the extradition – the deal the Director of Public Prosecutions (DPP) struck in order to get an unopposed extradition – were such that Anne and Bill could not be charged with any other offences. The charge was converted to a much lesser one of making a false declaration, and in September 1994 they pleaded guilty to this and were convicted and given a fine each of 5000 dollars. And that was the end of the road as far as the legal system was concerned. After six years of investigation the police had put up to the DPP many more briefs than this, but he chose only to go ahead with the one, after which of course the Hamilton-Byrnes could not be charged with anything else. We children had accepted quite a while before this that there was going to be little recompense or justice for us through the legal system. A lot of the abuse to which we had been subjected was under statutory limitation, which meant that Anne and Bill could not be prosecuted for it because too much time had elapsed between the event and the present time.

I feel that by writing this story I can at last tell the world about what really happened in Anne Hamilton-Byrne's Family, in a way that short snippets on the television or even my appearance as a witness in a court case could never even begin to address.

I want to tell my own story in this book – my story from my own point of view. I want to steer away from attempting to speak on behalf of the other children, for even though we shared much the same circumstances growing up in the cult, each one of us has a unique story of survival, and each of us has adapted to the world in an individual way and copes as best he or she can. Although we all agree on the basic facts of our life, I cannot and should not speak on the others' behalf about how it affected them. They value their privacy and thus I am changing their names to respect that, and will not speak of what they are doing now, for that is their own story.

Because mine was such a bizarre childhood of drugs and deprivation, it may be that I won't be able to remember every detail.

Yet all the events that I will describe *did* happen and I will try to recount them with honesty. I will tell the truth as best I can, though I know Anne and Bill Hamilton-Byrne and their followers will not want to hear the truth from one of us and they will say I'm lying or I'm mad.

When I was a child I was terrified of Anne, and when I was initiated into The Family and she became my guru that terror became a religious fear as well. When I first left the cult, it took a lot of courage even to have thoughts that challenged the conception that she was divine. I'm generally not scared of Anne any more, though sometimes the fear of her and her followers still grips me. The motto of the cult is 'Unseen, Unheard, Unknown', and even now the thought of the consequences of betraying that motto worries me at times. I've had death threats from cult members before. They may try to kill or hurt me for speaking out against Anne, though only on her direct orders. Many cult members have taken a vow to kill those who harm their Master. They will not walk up to me with a gun. But if I mysteriously drive over a cliff one night because my brakes are suddenly not working, or perish in a fire in my flat, they will be responsible.

I have just graduated as a doctor, but sometimes I think my medical career will be sabotaged because there are still many in the cult who have a lot of influence in professional and academic circles. It may sound melodramatic, but I know that some who were Anne's enemies have disappeared in strange circumstances. Yet I will have to risk her anger and hatred because I need to speak about what happened, to tell the story as it occurred. It is a story that must be told, because no one knows the truth of what happened except those of us who lived through it. If I do not write this book, the story will never be heard.

It is hard now for me to explain to others what it was like to live in The Family. Today The Family seems an alien world to me; often my experiences feel unreal, as if they had happened to someone else. It takes an effort to tap into the memories and the very different thought patterns that marked the way we used to exist. It takes courage to pierce the barrier of sanity and normality that I have had to erect in the last few years; a barrier created because, if I had continued to dwell in my memories and the consciousness created by the world we grew up in, I could not have functioned today as I do. Yet this story cannot be told without at least some painful memories being evoked, for without the pain there would have been no Uptop – our life would have been merely the harmless, slightly eccentric ideal that The Family always try to convey to the media.

I am not telling this story for revenge or because it is sensational. I am telling it because it is essential to the process of growing away from my past. This is a story that needs to be told, but it is in part also my attempt to come to terms with the reality that this, like it or not, was my past.

Perhaps, once I tell the story, I may be able to leave it behind me for good, and the nightmares may stop. Then I will finally be free of my childhood, finally perhaps be able to shed the shackles of fear and self-loathing that bound me to The Family for seventeen years. No longer will I have to be a prisoner or a victim. I can just get on and be me.

CHAPTER 1

Early on

I was five the first time I tried to die. Anne, my mother, was driving some of us in her big blue car to Kai Lama, on Lake Eildon, for the weekend.

As we entered the driveway of the house I opened the door and threw myself out of the moving car. I rolled to within centimetres of the back wheel. I hadn't been consciously planning to kill myself. I can't remember precisely what prompted me to do it at that instant: perhaps there had been another senseless belting or perhaps I just suddenly felt too miserable to want to live another moment. I thought that perhaps if the wheel crushed me, as I had seen happen to little rabbits and birds on the road, I would go to Heaven and be with Jesus. I'd heard that Jesus was always nice to little children. I'd heard that Jesus never hurt children.

I never did get to Heaven to find out if that was true. Instead the adults picked me up off the gravel and gave me a belting for opening the car door without permission. After that incident I wasn't allowed to sit near the door for many years. The adults were shocked and scandalised at what I had done, but they never thought to ask me why I did it; they just wouldn't let me sit near the door.

The year was 1974. In those days I was called Andrée. I had

lived the first four or five years of my life in a house called Winberra at Ferny Creek in the Dandenongs, the mountain range on the eastern rim of Melbourne. It was just one of many houses owned by my mother, Anne Hamilton-Byrne. It was a white, two-storey weatherboard house set on about 2 hectares of land. The grounds sloped down to a creek and were filled with tree ferns. I have vague memories of the sun filtering through them, of the greenness of the light.

Winberra had four bedrooms upstairs and two downstairs. In those days I shared an upstairs bedroom with Anna, who was about a year older than me. Anna is the first of my brothers and sisters I can clearly remember. Over the years the collection of children grew and the number of my siblings increased to about fourteen.

During our last year at Winberra, Anna and I went to Camberwell Girls' Grammar School. John, who was about two years older than me, attended the nearby boys' school called Kingswood College. Joy or John Travellyn, prominent members of the cult headed by my mother, usually drove us to school. I don't remember much about my life at this time and I don't even know how long I was a student at the school, although I think it was only a couple of months. I do remember that I was the smallest child in the grade, and that I could already read and write. I think I might have been the teacher's pet and I liked that.

Both Anna and I could read and write because all the children in The Family were taught how to at a very young age. School was both fun and easy for us. We were doing the work of older children and it made us feel good about ourselves. I loved the blue and white uniform, and especially the little straw hat we wore in summer.

Anna left the school before I did, after some sort of big row. I have a feeling it was something to do with her being accused of stealing food. I didn't know where she had gone – she just seemed to fade out of my life. Soon I was also taken away from Camberwell Girls' Grammar and I never went to school again. I can't remember exactly how old I was, though I would guess I was about five.

It was about this time that I started to spend most of my weekends at Kai Lama on Lake Eildon. To us the place became known simply as 'Uptop'. The house had been built on one of the many small promontories that jut into the lake and was surrounded on three sides by water. It was hidden in about 2 hectares of land on the left arm of Taylor Bay, about 8 kilometres from the town of Eildon. It was typical of a fairly small holiday-house, built of brown timber and set on a high point of the property. The rest of the land sloped away from the house towards the water.

Anna must have gone to Uptop when she left school, but I don't remember seeing her often. I remember her a year or so later, however, in about 1974, when I started living at Uptop permanently. She was there with me and the other children. I'm sure I never questioned where she had been. It was the way things were with people in my life – they came and went. Uptop became the one constant. I spent the next thirteen or so years of my life there, apart from several trips overseas, until 1987.

The rest of the children arrived at Uptop in dribs and drabs. Anna, Annette, Luke, Timothy and Stephen were the first to come. They came at about the same time that I did, having lived at Winberra with me when we were babies. Then Julieanne, two years younger than me, arrived, then Benjamin and Arrianne. These three had been looked after by prominent cult members until our mother decided that the time was right to bring them into The Family, whereupon their names were changed and they became Hamilton-Byrnes and brothers and sisters for the rest of us. The last of our brothers to arrive, Dallas (later called David), was very young, only about 2 or 3 years old. I remember he was always sick in the early days and covered with eczema from head to toe. Until about 1976 we were all Hamilton-Byrnes at Uptop, but after that a lot of other children came.

We called these other children 'fosters'. They were children who belonged to other cult members, as distinct from those of us who thought we were Hamilton-Byrnes. The fosters came to Uptop for various reasons: their parents may have been dispatched overseas on cult business, or they may have been told to separate by Anne, or the children may have been sent Uptop because they were hard to discipline. Still, the fosters were relatively lucky: they were able to leave, and growing up elsewhere in the cult was not nearly so harsh or isolated as living constantly Uptop. Some of the fosters who arrived at this time were Suzanne Omant, David K., Roland Whitaker, Jerome Stevenson, Jennifer and Carmel Macross, and Danielle and Cindy, whose surnames I don't remember.

There were also other fosters who stayed for varying lengths of time, but I can't think of their names. There were Austin, Aaron and Little Charlotte, who were brothers and sisters. They went back to the outside world for a period and then came up for another visit, and the boys' names were changed to Michael and Steve. They were younger than me. Another little girl called Madeleine stayed for a short while.

In about 1976, Susanne and Judith came to live Uptop. They were supposedly our cousins. They had an older brother, Shaun, who never stayed Uptop, but lived with the cult in England and still does. We were led to believe that these three were the children of Natasha, probably Anne's only biological daughter. Later we learnt that Susanne was an adopted child.

In 1978, Teresa, later called Andrea, came to live with us. At first she was called a Hamilton-Byrne, but after a while Anne changed her status to that of a cousin, 'sister' to Susanne and Judith. And in about 1980, Cassandra, the youngest in the family, came to live Uptop. Up to thirty children lived at Uptop in its heyday, although the fosters had varying lengths of stay. But the core group that stayed there all the time were Hamilton-Byrnes.

From the oldest to youngest we were John, Anna, Arrianne, Stephen, myself, Luke, Timothy, Andrea, Annette, Julieanne, Benjamin, David and Cassandra, plus Susanne and Judith, our cousins. All of us, apart from John, lived at Uptop for the majority of our childhood. John, our eldest brother, who was about four years older than me, never moved to Uptop from Winberra, but only visited at weekends. He went to live in England in 1982 and is still with the cult.

We were the children who formed Anne Hamilton-Byrne's 'family'. We believed ourselves to be the actual flesh and blood of Anne and her husband, Bill, and we called them Mummy and Daddy. Anne was the leader of a small cult in the Dandenongs called The Family or the Great White Brotherhood.

Possibly to explain why we were all so close in size and age, Anne created groupings of triplets and twins, which would be changed whenever it suited her. For example, I was a 'single' until I was about 7, then she decided that I was Stephen's twin. Stephen and I were very close at this time. He had been born congenitally blind and with a form of autism that meant he did not learn to speak until very late, and then in a very strange and stilted way. When we were living at Winberra and for some of the early years Uptop, I took him under my wing and used to lead him around and try to teach him the names of objects. I think because I had befriended him in this way Anne decided we should be called twins for a while. This lasted for about a year or two, then she decided I was a 'single' again. Finally, when I was 14, I became a triplet with Luke and Timothy.

Anne was always creative with our birthdays. Occasionally she would announce new birth dates, and often when we asked her how old we were she gave a different figure. By the time I was about 12 or so, I had been associated with almost every astrological sign in the zodiac!

Anne used to say that she couldn't remember the dates very well because she had so many children. Maybe in retrospect we should have realised that was weird, but when we were children we never thought it was anything out of the ordinary. Anne decided upon sets of twins and triplets, then gave us ages and birth dates to fit. We never questioned her. Birthday changes were just something we accepted. It was as if Anne knew so much more than us about

THE HAMILTON-BYRNE 'FAMILY TREE', 1994

everything that she just might be revealing another piece of our lifeplan when she changed our birthdays.

Uptop was our world and we were imprisoned within the confines of its boundaries. The land close to the house was cleared; the rest of the property was covered with weeds, scrub and the many large trees that had been planted by the cult to conceal the house from anyone on the lake. Near the house was a yard whose fence was topped with two layers of barbed wire, and there was another barbed wire fence surrounding the entire property. We had only this little yard in which to play; the rest of the property was forbidden to us.

THE UPPER LEVEL OF KAI LAMA

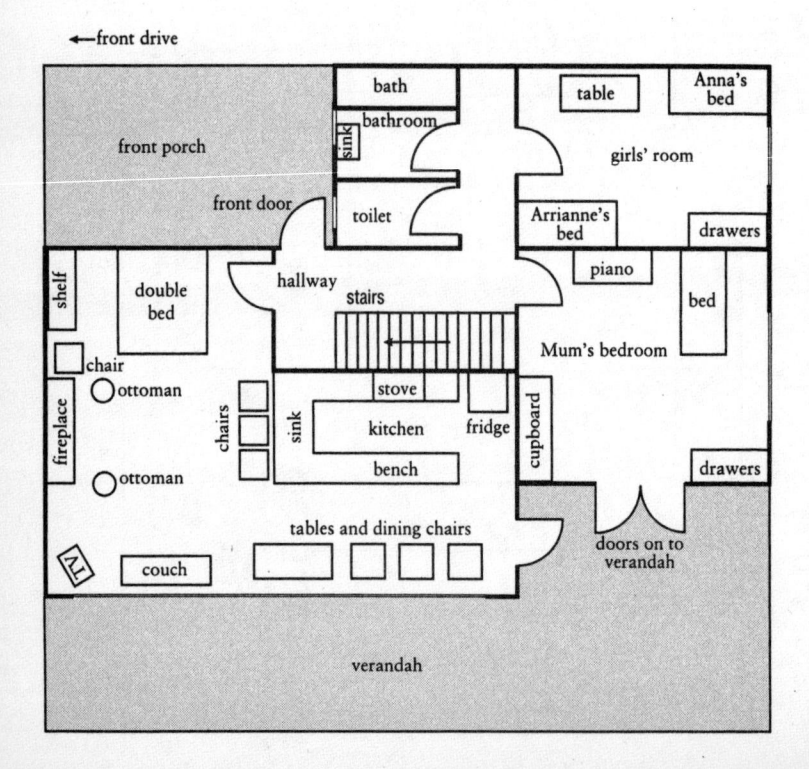

Early on 13

Inside the house, the lounge, dining-room and kitchen were all one L-shaped space and took up most of the upstairs area. We children ate at one large and three small tables that stretched along one side of the L. The kitchen was also in this part of the space and was fenced off by a little locked gate. The rest was a living area with a sofa and four armchairs in which we were not allowed to sit, save with express permission. There was also a double bed in this part of the room. This was the bed Anne and Bill slept in when they were in residence. When they came, the bed was made up with special sheets and draped with a ceremonial patchwork cover. A similar cover was placed over the couch. Usually, though,

THE LOWER LEVEL OF KAI LAMA

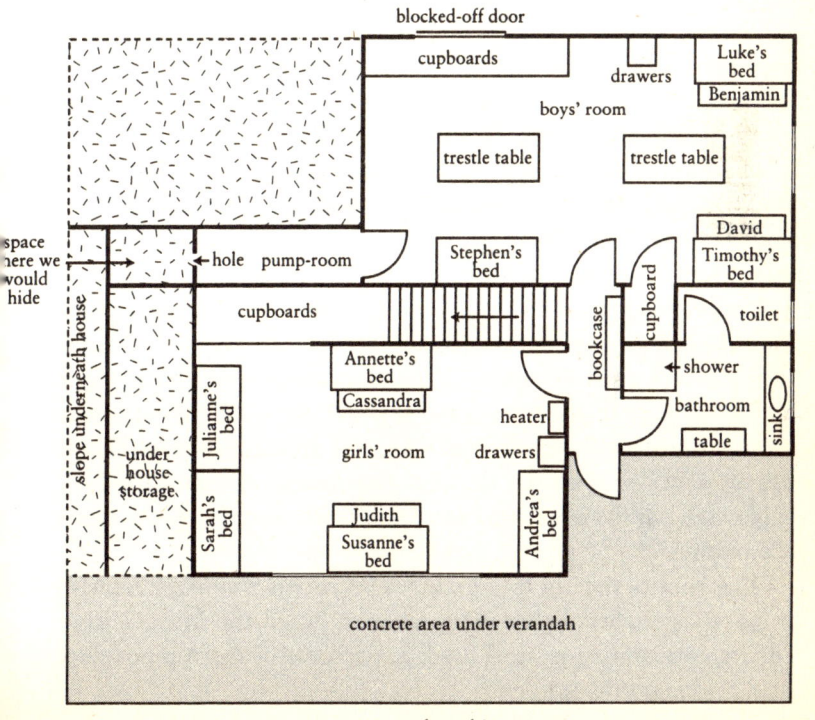

the bed and couch remained uncovered. Outside the lounge/dining-room area was a verandah that extended along the side of the house, forming the roof of a patio area on the lower level. Beyond the patio was our yard.

There were four bedrooms: two upstairs and two downstairs. One of the upstairs bedrooms was Anne's room although she didn't actually sleep there – it was where she kept her clothes and make-up, and there was also a piano. The other upstairs bedroom was a girls' room, where Arrianne and Anna slept. Downstairs there was another girls' bedroom and the boys' bedroom. The latter had been a boat-room and it doubled during the day as our schoolroom. In the early days this room had a concrete floor, which was later covered by lino and, in about 1980, by carpet.

I shared the downstairs girls' bedroom with the other girls. I remember sharing with Andrea (after 1978), Julieanne, Annette, Susanne, Cassandra (until 1986), and Judith. The foster girls also slept there when they were at Uptop, making up to thirteen girls sleeping in the one room. There were generally only about five or six boys plus a couple of Aunties in the boys' bedroom.

The Aunties were cult members rostered to look after us. Most were long-serving, inner-core members who, as part of their guru-seva (a Sanskrit term meaning 'service to the Master'), donated half their time to looking after us. They were rostered on at Uptop for a two-week period and then had two weeks off and went back to their outside jobs. In normal life all the Aunties were nurses, save one who was a school teacher. They were the people who brought us up, as most of the time Anne was not there. She spent about six months of every year in Australia, and during those months we usually saw her at weekends only. The Aunties taught us, fed us, supervised our lives and enforced Anne's rules and the punishments she outlined.

The Aunties slept in the children's bedrooms and in the lounge-room on stretchers. They slept there to guard the kitchen from children attempting to steal food. Later some of the Aunties slept in caravans on the property.

Lake Eildon is a favourite holiday destination but in all the time I lived Uptop I was never allowed to swim in the lake. I remember well on hot summer days looking out through the barbed-wire fence surrounding our yard and wishing I were allowed to swim in that cool water so tantalisingly close. We could often see and hear the weekend and holiday revellers having fun on the water in speed boats. We could count on one hand the number of times we were taken down to the lake by Bill and allowed to paddle as a special treat. On hot days, if Anne was Uptop, she might hose us down on the concrete under the verandah. This was considered a treat, mainly because we were spending quality time with Anne, but I would much rather have gone down to the lake. Like everything else in our lives, hosings were regimented. We'd be lined up in order of age and the hose would be splashed on us in turn. Generally we weren't allowed to simply run around and have fun: we had to stand still and receive the hosing.

I never even thought of asking to go for a swim. It was too presumptuous of children to ask for anything. Children were very inferior in the scheme of things, lower even than animals on the spiritual scale in Anne's teachings. Children were supposed to suffer to earn the right to become human beings. Children were supposed to be 'seen but not heard'. Apart from the punishments we received, the adults controlled us with the idea of privileges. If we were 'good' we might be granted a walk with Mummy, we might get an extra piece of fruit, we might receive a little present next time Mummy came home, we might even be allowed to speak to her for a little longer on the telephone. We were manipulated all the time.

Going outside the property was one of the privileges held out to us. If we did extra work and did it quickly or if the Aunties, in their report to Anne when she visited, said that we had all been good, we might go on one of 'Mummy's walks'. We might go with her and Bill or with Uncle Leon or one of the Aunties.

Once, when I was about 12, we went for a walk with Anne and I saw a man standing with a gun on the bank above us. Anne had told us on numerous occasions that the bush around Eildon was full of escaped convicts, rapists and murderers, and that if we left the property we'd be tortured and killed by the men in the hills. When I saw the man with the gun I took it as proof of her warnings. I was terrified and so were some of the others, although now I think he was probably just a rabbit hunter. Anne was yelling at us to get into a line behind her, threatening to kill us if we disobeyed, and I don't think she saw the armed figure, but he must have heard her for he disappeared at the sound of her voice. I was deeply impressed with the power of our mother – able to scare away madmen, able to protect her brood.

CHAPTER 2

A day in my life

I find a lot of my childhood hard to remember. Very few incidents stand out for me. I remember what our routine was but I don't remember many individual days. I think this is because we had none of the normal milestones that mark the passing of the years for other children. We never changed grades or teachers. We almost never celebrated birthdays (I can recall only about three such occasions), and Christmas and Easter were acknowledged infrequently, perhaps with presents if Anne and Bill were there. Life went on and looking back it seems that the only memorable times were particularly violent ones. I try to remember things other than beatings and bad times and it's quite hard. There must have been long periods when nothing in particular happened, bad or good, and we may have had ordinary child-like feelings of fun and excitement then, but these are mostly forgotten.

There is one thing I do remember about my childhood. I remember darkness. I remember that light was something I treasured. I remember how Anne hated bright lights and that none of the globes in the overhead lights were allowed to be more than 20 watts. How the windows were heavily curtained. How dull things were. I didn't know it could have been brighter inside. Years later one of the things our police rescuers commented on was the darkness of the place.

There was no generator when we first arrived Uptop and it was not until the early 1980s, when I was about 12 or 13, that we got mains electricity. Before that event light came from little gas lamps and the gas was rationed in those dark days of childhood. Later the lights ran from a generator during the main part of the day and we used gas light at night and in the early mornings.

Before the electricity was connected we had only watched television on the rare occasions when we were overseas. In fact, before the connection to mains electricity I don't think I even knew that television existed in Australia. We were in complete isolation Uptop. We didn't understand where we were, least of all that we were close to Melbourne, a city of three million people. We had no concept of what a city was, or of any human community other than the one in which we existed.

When I was little I thought that 'overseas' was the other side of the lake, and that that was where Mummy and Daddy were when they went away. As instructed by the Aunties, we used to wave out the window to them at night before we went to sleep. Although we ourselves travelled overseas several times we did not really have any understanding of the distance travelled. We were aware of driving along a road, hopping on a plane, getting off, entering a waiting car and driving to one of Anne's properties in the United States or England. That was it. We weren't allowed to see newspapers until we were quite a bit older and even then they'd been censored – we were only allowed to look at the sports section, and then only if we begged, as we loved cricket.

Until about 1986 all the children at Uptop were dressed alike, with matching hairstyles, tied with identical-coloured ribbons. The hair of most of the girls was dyed blonde, cut in a fringe at the front and worn long at the back. All the boys had basin haircuts.

Aunty Wynn made our clothes. The girls wore smocks, which were made of gingham or cotton. They were checked, in pink, yellow, red and blue, and were handed down from the older children to the younger ones. They were all the same style and under them we wore identical-coloured jumpers or skivvies. We had to wear the same colours at the same time, and for about two days at a time. When we weren't wearing the smocks, and at night, we had to hang them on coat hangers above Annette's bed or in the cupboard according to colour and in the order of our ages.

The boys also wore identical jumpers or skivvies, usually blue or red. They did not have smocks. We all wore jeans, which were washed and changed about once every two months. We also all had blue and white tracksuits, which we wore to do Hatha yoga and on weekends. When we were young we had identical little red shoes. About 1980, Anne bought us all blue and white runners.

In the early days Uptop, before the connection to mains electricity, the Aunties had to wash everything by hand with water that was carried to the house from the lake in buckets. For this reason they hated it if we got our clothes dirty. Getting our smocks dirty – almost impossible to avoid – was a major crime, punishable by a belting or at least the missing of one meal. We were continually acquiring fruit stains on our clothing, in particular, due to all the fruit we ate.

The practice of hair bleaching started when we were quite young, and continued throughout our years at Kai Lama. The bleaching was of course at Anne's direction and was done by Aunty Wynn every month. It was a lengthy process. Aunty Wynn used a paint brush to apply the stuff from out of a purple bottle, and a shower cap had to be worn for a couple of hours, which looked really stupid. Most of the children had their hair dyed; only about five of us escaped. However, the overall impression anyone who met us as a group gained was that we were all blond, cloned from our mother. This impression was accentuated by the fact we were all dressed identically.

Anne bleached my hair only once. The stuff stung like mad. I was otherwise left alone because, for some reason, my red hair was acceptable. We never knew as young children that this 'protein treatment', as it was euphemistically referred to, meant that our hair was being dyed. We thought it was being specially cleaned; it was only much later, when we compared ourselves with other children, that we realised our hair must have been dyed white.

At Uptop we were given daily doses of tranquillisers to 'calm us down' and I think these took the edge off everything – that, plus the sheer monotony and sameness of our existence and the fact we weren't allowed off the property. As well, the long punishment schedules, which might go on for many months, tended to make us lose our perspective and also our sense of time. Time tended to run into itself; we lost sight of all boundaries.

This was our weekday routine.

6.00 a.m.	Rise (in summer at 5.00 a.m.). Wash and dress, with showers for girls and boys on alternate days. Make the beds.
6.30–7.30 a.m.	Practise Hatha yoga.
7.30–7.45 a.m.	Listen to Anne's doctrines on tape or to Baba Muktananda on tape.
7.45–8.00 a.m.	Chant mantras.
8.00–8.15 a.m.	Meditate.
8.15–8.30 a.m.	Set up the schoolroom. Run or do physical exercises. Get dressed in smocks and jeans.
8.30–9.00 a.m.	Have breakfast of fruit.
9.00–10.45 a.m.	Do schoolwork.
10.45–11.00 a.m.	Have a break.
11.00–12.30 p.m.	Do schoolwork.
12.30–1.30 p.m.	Meditate or play spaceball. Have lunch of steamed vegetables and fruit. Have a break or do homework.
1.30–2.45 p.m.	Do schoolwork.
2.45–3.00 p.m.	Have a break.
3.00–4.00 p.m.	Do schoolwork.
4.00–5.00 p.m.	Pack up the schoolroom, clean the rooms, shower.

5.00–5.20 p.m.	Meditate.
5.20–6.00 p.m.	Have tea (usually a bland vegetarian meal).
6.00–6.30 p.m.	Read spiritual works.
6.30–9.00 p.m.	Do homework.
9.00 p.m.	Go to bed (latest bedtime for oldest children).

A normal day at Uptop began at 6 o'clock (5 o'clock in summer) with the alarm clock going off upstairs in the lounge-room where Aunty Helen slept on guard against food thieves. Aunty Helen would come stumbling downstairs, guided by torch light, and go first to the boys' bedroom to wake up Aunty Liz or Aunty Trish who slept there. They would lurch out to the bathroom and get dressed.

Aunty Helen would light the gas light in the boys' room and go around checking the boys' beds to see who had wet them the night before. The poor children guilty of this would be led by the ear into the bathroom to have a belting administered by Aunty Trish or Aunty Liz. Then they would be shoved, still in their pyjamas, under a cold shower, no matter how freezing the weather outside. Thus every morning of my childhood I awoke to the sounds of children howling as they got their first belting for the day. Rare was the day that no one wet the bed, at least until 1986, and even then the younger boys continued to do so on occasions.

The unfortunate bed-wetters had to wash their own sheets during breakfast, and often had to miss lunch as well. The sheets were piled in a corner of the bathroom until breakfast time and they smelled horrible.

After dealing with the boys, Aunty Helen would come in and light the gas light in the girls' bedroom, for which task she had to stand on Annette's bed. The mantle of the light always seemed to be broken. If it wasn't, it lit with a 'pouf' and sent out an eerie, uncertain light. We were always awake – due to the alarm – so we had those few minutes while the boys were being woken to enjoy bed for a bit longer. Once Helen had lit the light we had to leap into action, otherwise the bedclothes would be torn off us and it would take a lot longer to make our beds. Beds had to be made very neatly with 'nurse's corners'. As we did not have much time, the older ones helped the little ones to make their beds as quickly as possible.

Then the stretchers were folded and put in one corner and the trundle beds rolled under the higher beds so that the centre of the room was cleared. Usually at night the floor of the girls' room was completely covered with beds. We had to walk along the edges of the beds to get out to the toilet, which action, by the way, was usually forbidden as was any movement out of bed at night, although in view of the number of wet beds this rule had to be relaxed. (In an attempt to forestall bed-wetting one of the Aunties would come downstairs at about 10 o'clock in the evening, wake the boys up and take them to the toilet. It usually didn't work.)

After the beds were made in the morning, we filed into the bathroom two by two, the girls going after the boys, to wash our faces, drink a glass or more of water, brush our teeth, and go to the toilet. In winter we usually had to have a spoonful of cod liver oil, supervised by one of the Aunties.

Also, once a week, or more if it was considered that an individual had a weight problem, we were weighed and the results entered in a book to be communicated later to Anne. She had a horror of fatness and was obsessed with body shape and weight. She always insisted that we girls were getting too fat, even though in some cases it was malnutrition rather than extra kilos that caused our bellies to stick out.

Weighing was a very serious business – particularly serious for us because if it was considered that we were putting on too much weight we would have our food rations cut down and that was a dreadful proposition, food being the most important thing in our lives. We girls viewed the scales with hatred. They made our miserable lives even worse. Some of the girls would even try to induce vomiting on weighing mornings in an attempt to seem lighter.

A few of the girls showered in the morning if there was time. We showered every two days in a rostered system, some in the morning and some at night. We were allowed a maximum of three minutes under the shower with strict instructions about 'No washing down there!'. We were forbidden to look at our bodies under the shower – we were supposed to wash with our eyes shut – and we were also ordered not to look at anyone else. Particularly forbidden was any contact between girls and boys in the bathroom. I do believe that I had not seen a naked male body – even in a book, as these, too, were heavily censored – until I studied Year Twelve biology after I had escaped from the cult. In summer, when water was scarce, we often couldn't shower and had to wash from a bucket, or else the bath would be filled and all of us had to use it. The water was pretty dark and scungy by the time it was the turn of the last few.

After washing or showering we had to be on the floor in position for Hatha yoga by 6.30 at the latest. Hatha lasted for an hour, during which we followed a prescribed order of four main asanas (positions) interspersed with minor exercises and relaxation. Most of the girls did yoga in their bedroom; those who could not squeeze in joined the boys in their room.

As we did yoga every day of our lives from a very young age, we were extremely supple and able to bend over backwards and stand on our heads for long periods of time. Indeed we had a sort of competition to see who could hold the headstand the longest before fainting. Eventually we were given red towels on which to do our yoga; before this we laid out blankets, which slipped about on the lino. We lay on the floor side by side, about half a metre between us. The children of one row positioned themselves between the children in the next to form staggered rows. Each person had a specific place and one child, who lay perpendicular to the rest at the front, acted as supervisor and directed the pace of the exercises and kept the time.

Hatha yoga finished at about 7.20 and the girls then picked up the towels. Yoga was often the only exercise we got for the day, especially during the long periods when we were totally confined indoors. This happened when there were people in the vicinity or some suspected media or police interest. It could go on for many months. Or we could be confined simply as punishment.

While we were doing our yoga, most of the Aunties were upstairs having their breakfast. *They* got tea and toast. They also read a daily affirmation from a book called *God Calling*. Sometimes one Aunty was left downstairs to keep an eye on us or to wash our clothes.

While there were times when we liked yoga, it was mostly very boring, and if we could fool around or sleep instead we would. However, since an Aunty was usually supervising downstairs or listening upstairs in order to rush down and catch us out, there was little escape; we usually had to do all of the yoga. Nevertheless, on any occasion when we felt the Aunties were distracted upstairs, we would stop practising. Because we could hear their movements above us, we generally had plenty of time to get back into our positions before they got even half-way down the stairs. One person was often posted as a lookout and would stage-whisper, '*Aunties coming!*', when movement was heard above.

Aunty Liz and Aunty Wynn would sometimes try to catch us out by creeping down the stairs or outside under the windows; if they did catch us there would be severe punishments. Aunty Trish knew we mucked around but, unless she was in a particularly bad mood, she didn't make it an issue, although obviously if she actually caught us at it she was compelled to punish us. When we felt enthusiastic about Hatha yoga, there was pleasure in doing it well, and we were proud to demonstrate how good we were to Anne on her visits. But, like children everywhere, our interest in doing the same thing every day was hard to maintain.

After yoga we all went into the boys' room, and the Aunties came downstairs. We sat cross-legged on the floor and the room was darkened. Incense was lit and for fifteen minutes we listened to a tape of Anne preaching. These tapes were recordings of her speeches to the disciples of the cult, given on weekly Thursday evening darshans (a word meaning 'meeting with the Master'). All the darshans were faithfully recorded, making up a large library of tapes for us and the other cult members to listen to and study. Anne spoke on various topics, such as Love and Brotherhood, about kundalini (Divine Energy) and different forms of yoga, and about how best to think and perform and live one's life as a good disciple. Each tape was on a different topic and we would listen to the same one over and over for about four weeks.

On alternate days, we listened to tapes of Baba Muktananda instead. He was an Indian sanyassin/swami, who had attained enlightenment and become a guru (teacher) in the Siddha yoga tradition. We first met Baba in 1978, when I was about 8 years old. He was over from India on the second of his world tours to spend time teaching at his ashram in Fitzroy. I'm not sure how Anne heard of him or whether she'd met him before that but we girls were taken on a trip down to Melbourne to meet him. Later that year Anna, Arrianne and myself went over to Hawaii and spent some time at his ashram, living right by his house for a few months and seeing him every day. We visited him again, in the Catskill Mountains, in New York State, in 1979 and 1981.

Meeting Baba changed our lives. We absolutely loved him. He was kind. He lavished on us his love and attention. He treated us as special, as human beings in our own right. He was the first person who ever gave us something unconditionally, and he completely won us over.

I thought he was marvellous. To be shown kindness by an adult was almost unheard of. We were so starved of love that when he showed us affection he had our devotion for ever. We revered and loved Baba for most of our childhood: he became a major influence in our lives. We studied many of his teachings and I became a convert to the spiritual path that he taught. We learnt in the ashram how to sing the Sanskrit chants and the Sri Guru Gita, which is a song of reverence to the guru in the form of a conversation between Parvati and the god Shiva. We continued this practice with great devotion when we returned to Australia. I accepted and worshipped Baba as a divine Master and self-realised being, and, unlike Anne, he never gave me any reason to doubt his authenticity.

Baba paid us children and Anne a lot of attention when we were with him. I remember when we were in the Catskills he would ride over on his golf-buggy from his ashram and house just down the road from us, to talk to us in the mornings. He spoke Hindi and had an English translator. He would give us rides in his golf-buggy and laugh, sing with us, and pinch our cheeks in affection. We also had many private darshans with him, where he would talk and laugh with us and give us presents and lollies. He took a great interest in us children and I think Anne was jealous of the attention he paid us. Baba is one of my few good memories, and meeting him was, without doubt, the best thing that ever happened in my childhood.

At Uptop our daily fifteen minutes of listening to Baba or Anne on tape was followed by fifteen minutes of chanting. We usually chanted Sanskrit mantras or parts of the Sri Guru Gita. After the chanting we meditated for twenty to twenty-five minutes, depending on the time.

By 8.15 we were ready to set up the schoolroom. This involved carrying in trestle tables and folding chairs from outside, arranging them in the boys' bedroom and taking our school bags out of a locked cupboard. Then, if we had done all this quickly and had enough time before school, we went out to the yard and did exercises for ten to fifteen minutes. These consisted of jogging on the spot, leg raises, hopping, frog jumping and running around the perimeter of the yard outside the house – probably a distance of 100 metres. Occasionally we were allowed to run up and down to the gate – again a distance of 100 metres. At all other times we had to have permission to leave the yard. It was a serious offence if we were caught outside it. It was fenced with chicken wire, with barbed wire on top of that, to a height of 2 metres in some places, although there were sections of the fence that only had wire to a height of a metre or so. As well as this top yard there was a bottom yard separated from it by a gate. In the bottom yard were some monkey bars, which we were allowed to play on occasionally, although when we girls got older this activity was discouraged as 'unladylike'.

More important than the fences imprisoning us was our ignorance and fear of what lay in wait for us in the outside world. We didn't think of running away because we did not know enough about what was out there. We were taught to be frightened of the 'evil outside world', of everything beyond the big brown gate that guarded the property.

The top yard had a concrete area under the verandah, which was often the only area we were allowed to play in because it was not visible from the water. The rest of the yard was covered with gravel, and there was a small hill with a few trees. On one side was a cacti rock-garden, which went up the side of the hill to above the level of the girls' bedroom window. The boundaries of the yard marked the extent of our exploration of the outside world, except for our rare walks outside the property or up to the gate. I knew every stone, every rock and the pattern of the bark on every tree in that yard.

I also knew the parts of the fence that could be jumped over to gain access to the rest of the property if, for example, a ball was lost. As I have said, this was strictly forbidden, but if someone just quickly ran down the slope beyond and back up, he or she was usually not caught. It was a huge adrenaline rush, however, with the fear of the consequences of getting caught.

At about 8.30 a.m., after our exercises, there was breakfast. This was always three pieces of fruit (four for the boys) – usually an apple, orange and banana or pear. The Aunties had a deal to buy cases of 'seconds' from a local orchard. Often the fruit was rotten as a new batch was only brought up fortnightly. It was boring eating the same thing for breakfast every day of our life, and fruit was not very filling or comforting on cold mornings. Still, we were grateful for it: we had learnt not to complain about our food.

Breakfast didn't take long and, as Aunty Helen rang the school bell for assembly at 9 o'clock, we didn't dawdle. Assembly consisted of a roll-call. We lined up on the concrete outside the back door in order of age and trooped in one by one. If someone spoke or shuffled during assembly he or she got an instant smack from Aunty Helen's ruler. The edge of a ruler especially hurt the knuckles on a brisk morning and we would shake and blow on them to try to ease the pain.

School usually began with spelling – words and their meanings from the day before had had to be memorised for testing. When we were young, those who made a spelling mistake were smacked over the hand with a ruler or were occasionally hauled up before the front of the class, made to bend over the oil heater and pull down their pants and were belted with the metre ruler. Needless to say, I always did very well in spelling. Andrea, then known as Teresa, was once pulled up and beaten for writing too slowly to keep up with the rest of us.

Our school life, under the instruction of Aunty Helen, was rigid. Kai Lama wasn't registered by the State government as a school until 1984. Before then, we weren't supposed to be there during the week. We were hidden when visitors or tradespeople came to the house. As far as the authorities were concerned, we went to schools in Melbourne, so a lot of effort went into hiding us from visitors.

Teaching at Uptop concentrated on multiplication tables, spelling and writing. We had to learn an old-fashioned style of writing, similar to cursive script. We had books with three ruled lines to keep our writing to a certain size. We practised writing letters for pages and pages until they were perfect. It was a painstaking task trying to keep within those lines and we were rapped over the knuckles by Aunty Helen or Aunty Margot if we made a mistake.

We all did spelling, but after that we would be set tasks that were relevant to our age. We were all at different levels in maths and other subjects. I have to thank the Aunties for the basis of my education. When we were young they drummed reading and writing and multiplication tables into us and the grounding has stood me in good stead.

Despite everything else that happened, they gave us one of the greatest gifts adults can bestow upon children – literacy and language skills. They taught us basic French and some primary school geography. They could only really teach us to primary school level, except in the case of maths where, under the weekend tuition of Leon Dawes, we were doing Year Ten, Eleven and Twelve work at really young ages.

Uncle Leon taught maths at a high school in Croydon during the week, and all weekend, every weekend, he enthusiastically imparted to us a sophisticated knowledge and love of mathematics. He believed in starting kids off at the deep end, so at an early age we were learning algebra and calculus.

Leon also taught us a smattering of German and chemistry and we learnt a little Latin from Aunty Trish. In later years, after Helen and Trish had taught us all they could, we were left much to our own devices. Leon brought up textbooks pinched from Croydon High and we were left to work at our own pace through these. It was a hit and miss education. Only a couple of us actually got much out of it because self-education suits very few people.

In some subjects such as maths we were precociously advanced, in others we were woefully inadequate. There were great gaps in our schooling. Even when I reached university I found some things difficult because there was an assumption of knowledge that I simply had not acquired. It may seem bizarre to some that I have been able to get through a university course, but Medicine is a specialised science taught largely from scratch and I found the anomalies in my early schooling only caused me trouble on rare occasions. I suppose if I had chosen to study Arts or Politics or even Science, I would not have coped so well, as we knew little or nothing about these things.

At 10.45 a.m. we had a break for fifteen minutes. What we were allowed to do during this time depended on what was going on in the house. Often we were only allowed outside two at a time because of the risk of strangers seeing us from the lake and reporting to the authorities that there were children there during the week.

I remember how, on hot summer days during our breaks, we would stand at the yard fence and gaze through the thick screen of trees at the water glinting in the sun. I would usually be sent out for a break with Megan or, in later years, with Andrea, who became my best friend. However, friendships were frowned upon by Anne and children could be punished for getting too chummy. At one time, during a punishment period that lasted twelve months, Andrea and I were forbidden to speak to each other. Boys and girls were also prevented from playing together.

In the later years we had to play spaceball in our breaks, although if there were a few of us outside together we would much rather have played tiggy or poison ball or cricket. Sometimes, if there was no security risk, we were all allowed outside together, or first the girls then the boys. Often we were only allowed outside together on weekends. Football was banned as being too unladylike for the girls and too much of a risk to the windows. If we were confined to the concrete we played hopscotch, skipped or chased each other round and round the small area, which measured only about 10 metres by five.

Certain things were forbidden outside. We were not allowed to raise our voices; in fact sometimes we were forbidden from talking at all. Other things that were forbidden were fighting, picking up sticks or stones, playing in the dirt, omitting to pack away under the house any balls or playthings used, dropping any rubbish, and boys playing near girls. The list was endless.

Any writing of lines as a punishment had to be done during break times, and offenders were also kept in if they got spelling wrong, talked during school, had to go to the toilet outside break times, or were caught passing notes or looking at another child's work. Aunty Helen used to imitate a special bird whistle to call us in at the end of break. Much later, when we were teenagers, and began to object to being whistled at like dogs, she rang a bell.

After the break there was more schoolwork until 12.30 p.m.

Then, when spaceball was fashionable with the Aunties (that is, when Anne had made a particular fuss about it), we got a further ten minutes of it.

Spaceball was a game approved of by Anne: in fact it was said that she invented it. It was supposed to 'unite body and soul' and make us feel really bright. Basically we stood in a circle and threw a ball around to each other in patterns as fast as we could. It came into our lives in about 1982 and after that we had to spend our breaks playing it. It got boring and I got annoyed with it. I used to try to get out of doing it as much as possible. Anne thought that it improved our mental capacity and told us that 'Israel University' had devised something similar for its students.

If we didn't do spaceball, we went up to the lounge-room and practised singing or speech. We were taught speech by Aunty Lillibet who came up on Wednesdays. She also taught us piano and singing. Anne wanted us to speak like well-bred English children, and we practised saying vowels so that we wouldn't sound Australian.

After that there was lunch. It was always steamed or boiled vegetables – carrot, pumpkin, parsnip, turnip, squash, and potato, our favourite. We got a plate of these followed by a piece of fruit for dessert. Usually the vegetables were reasonable, although all our food was unsalted and unflavoured except for an oil and vinegar dressing on salads. However, if a lot of us were missing lunches due to punishments, the vegetables were reboiled day after day and served up again. As you can imagine, they ended up pretty tasteless and mushy. Generally lunch was the most filling and satisfying meal of the day so to miss it was considered by us to be a true privation.

Depending on how long it took to eat lunch, we had time to play until 1.30 p.m., usually fifteen to twenty minutes. From 1.30 to 2.45 we did more schoolwork, then had another break until 3 o'clock, followed by another hour's school. At 4 o'clock we packed up and dismantled the schoolroom. Between 4 and 5 o'clock we had to clean the rooms, have showers or baths and, when we got older, wash our clothes.

The rooms had to be spotless – there was often an inspection before tea. During an inspection we had to stand to attention at the foot of our beds while the Aunties checked how well they were made, whether the carpet was spotless, whether the socks and underwear were neatly folded in geometric shapes in the drawers, whether the shelves and the objects on them had been dusted, whether the clothes in the cupboard were folded in identical-sized piles, and whether the smocks were hung in the correct order.

We were very industrious at cleaning the rooms and we took great pride in presenting ourselves well at these inspections and tried to get praise from the Aunties and Anne and Bill. We girls used to help out the boys, because, like boys everywhere, they were not as good at getting things tidy.

From 5 o'clock to 5.20 we did more meditation, sitting cross-legged in set positions on the lounge-room floor. Then we had tea, which was usually salad, or yoghurt once a week, scrambled eggs once in a blue moon, rice occasionally, or jelly or fruit salad in summer. This was followed by two or three biscuits, a handful of nuts and sultanas occasionally, and one or two pieces of fruit.

At 6 o'clock we did spiritual reading – reading from the Indian scriptures – for example, from the Bhagavad Gita (the conversation of the great warrior Arjuna with the god Krishna, which had lots of spiritual principles and advice for living), from the Puranas or Upanishads or from various discourses about them. We also read from the works of Baba Muktananda (our favourites were books called *Satsang with Baba*, where disciples asked questions and he answered them with parables and advice, which I read over and over and knew virtually by heart), from the writings of Shri Chinmoy, Sri Ramakrishna Paramahansa, Sai Baba, Meher Baba, Rajneesh and others. Sometimes, too, we read from the Bible or books discussing it.

One person would also read a passage out loud and then we would discuss it and be asked questions by the Aunties about it.

This went on for about half an hour, after which the younger ones were sent to bed and the older ones put up one of the trestle tables and did homework.

Nine o'clock was the latest bedtime for the oldest kids. Nine o'clock was lights out time and any noise or movement after that was punishable by missing meals the next day.

Weekends were more relaxed. We got up at 7 o'clock, did the yoga and meditation routine for two hours, or sometimes longer, especially if Anne was there. We then did schoolwork with Uncle Leon until 11 o'clock, when we had brunch, a special weekend treat, which was a bowl of muesli or porridge, fruit, two or three biscuits, a handful of nuts and sultanas and occasionally some cheese or an egg. Alternatively, we could have as much fruit as we could eat. Weekend food was much better than weekday food, and it was terrible if you had to miss brunch as a punishment.

After brunch we did maths with Leon with a few breaks until between 6 and 7 o'clock when we had tea. We did not have homework on weekends and sometimes, in the later years, we were allowed to watch an educational video that Leon brought with him. Sometimes he would bring up a more entertaining video such as *Robin Hood* but nothing too racy was allowed. The Aunties had their fingers on the stop button and they would 'fast forward' through scenes of sex or violence.

After the television arrived we hardly ever watched it because it was considered a privilege and we always lost privileges as punishment. We got the video recorder in the early 1980s. On rare occasions Trish allowed us to watch the cricket as a treat. On Saturday nights, when we were younger, we sometimes played chess or draughts or Chinese checkers, supervised of course. When Anne and Bill were 'home', one of our favourite treats was watching projector super-eight films.

This was our routine and it never varied while I was Uptop. Every day was totally predictable. It is easy to understand why one of my strongest childhood impressions is the sameness of things, broken now and again by fads. There were enduring constants: we were always in trouble, and we were always being punished although the methods changed. I remember the rigid routine of our life as a march: it went on and on.

It is hard for other people to imagine just how monotonous the routine was. Events others take for granted as part of daily life – a day in the park, a trip to the zoo, a visit to family or friends, a sudden decision to postpone a chore and do something different – simply did not happen. A trip to the cinema or an impromptu swim in the lake on a hot summer's evening was out of the question. Day in, day out, year after year, for all the time we stayed up there, the pattern of life remained the same.

Looking back, I can see that any game or hobby we started we would get hooked on, playing it over and over again in our limited spare time. If we got into a game or fantasy, it assumed the utmost importance in our lives.

To an outsider it might have appeared that we were obsessive kids, but our obsessiveness was understandable considering the malevolent reality we faced outside our games. Usually Anne and the Aunties saw to it that, as soon as we started enjoying a particular activity, it was stopped, and a new rule would be made, forbidding us to play that game. We would thus be forced to try to make up a new one within the boundaries of the rules that governed our lives, knowing that eventually this new one, too, would be banned. This was what happened when I developed a private game to overcome my feelings of isolation.

Despite all the brothers and sisters I had, I was a very lonely child. I loved reading and immersed myself in the stories of any new books that found their way Uptop. Aunty Helen used to borrow books from a library in town for us. They were carefully censored: we weren't allowed to read anything that might corrupt us, particularly anything to do with sex or relationships. I loved the Narnia books by C. S. Lewis when I was young. I was inspired by the struggle between good and evil.

If I was not able to read, I took refuge in my imagination. When I was about 6 or 7, I had a kingdom of my own, which I called

Fairyland. This was my own world where only good things happened, where I was in charge and nothing bad could get to me. I could have anything my imagination could create. Here, I was the queen and I controlled my little land with care. I created and ruled this kingdom with Megan, who at that time was my best friend and playmate and shared my vivid imagination. It took all morning break to inspect the royal horses and stables. Sitting on my imaginary pure white charger, hair flying in the wind, I rode around and around the edges of my kingdom, whose borders were the wire fences of the yard at Kai Lama.

Eventually I got into trouble for my imagination; we always got into trouble for anything we started to enjoy too much. What happened was a good example of the way our lives were completely regimented and controlled. I was talking on my 'phone', a chain hanging from a stump in the bottom yard, issuing orders for delicate negotiations with emissaries from the neighbouring kingdom, when a few of the boys saw me and began taunting me.

Inevitably, the story of my game got back to Anne. She was enraged. She decided that Megan and I were imagining that there were naked people in Fairyland and this, allegedly, revealed our base and sluttish nature and was proof that our play had something to do with sex. She made these accusations even though we were only about 6 years old. Megan and I were hauled up before everyone and given 'the treatment' by our mother. She publicly humiliated us and we were interrogated until we recanted. We were then punished. The public exposé meant that the game was over forever, wrecked by Anne's half-crazed accusations. We were ordered never to play it again – not that we would have wanted to after that – and we were belted for our wicked thoughts. More sinister was the fact that we were labelled by Anne from then on as troublemakers.

The infliction of public humiliation was a speciality of Anne's and such scenes were a big part of my childhood. At the slightest hint of ego or pride, Anne and her adult daughter, Natasha, would grind us into the dust. They were masters of the public taunting.

When I was young I was completely intimidated and cowed by it, like everyone else. It was not until I became a teenager that I finally learnt how to cope with it. I learnt that you had to fight back and act as if you didn't care what they said about you. Agree with their jibes and mock them.

'You're a lesbian because you walk like a man', Anne would jeer when I was about sixteen.

'Well, maybe I am. Who cares?' was the best answer (even though I had no idea at the time what a lesbian was: I just knew that it was considered by Anne to be something bad). If you allowed an embarrassed silence to grow around you they went in for the kill.

Only an extraordinary event, or a rare special dispensation from Anne, or one of our trips overseas could change even an hour of the day at Uptop. The major event that punctuated our lives was the comings and goings of Anne and Bill. We always seemed to be waiting for them to arrive. If they were delayed for any reason, it was inevitably us who received the blame.

Sometimes, when she was up on weekends, Anne would stay until Monday, and on those days we would have a different routine. Usually the whole day would be devoted to spiritual pursuits, and we would spend many hours studying the religious books, meditating and chanting. Frequently these were wonderfully enjoyable days, but too often she would use the opportunity to punish us for wrongdoings that the Aunties had reported, and occasionally she would fly into one of her unpredictable rages or decide that we needed more rules or discipline, which prompted her to write some further instructions in her rule books.

Even from a childhood such as mine, a few good memories emerge. Cricket, like the times spent in spiritual pursuits, was one of them. Aunty Trish introduced us to the game. We first started playing with an old bat of Leon Dawes. There were enough of us to ensure that there were always plenty of fielders. The summers we were allowed to play cricket stand out from the sameness of the rest of the time. We still received beltings and missed meals, were given lines and were spied on by the Aunties, and took the blame for everything that went wrong, but at least we had a bit of fun.

Playing cricket enabled us to be more like normal kids than at any other time. I remember getting annoyed with the little ones for not being much good at batting, but on the whole I was good natured when I was playing cricket. I could just relax and be a kid and I loved it. Most of the rest of the time was taken up with feeling responsible, guilty and worried.

Some days after school, instead of tidying our rooms, we were allowed to go outside for a while to play. Such an activity at that time of day wasn't on any of the lists stipulating how we were to spend our time. It was an unexpected bonus given to us by Aunty Trish, and for that I am grateful to her. She even convinced Anne to let us watch a little cricket on television. I remember the day-night games and barracking for New Zealand (because at that time that is where I thought I had been born). Richard Hadlee, Lance Cairns and the Crowe brothers were my idols. The others admired Dennis Lillee, Rod Marsh and Allan Border. In this, we were very like other children.

And then the inevitable happened. Luke was a fast bowler and a window got broken by an errant ball. The bat was confiscated and we weren't allowed to play any more, or even to watch the game on television. Anne said it was too vulgar. As usual this punishment wasn't a normal discipline where a child might be banned temporarily from doing something before being given another chance. No: we were banned from playing cricket for twelve months. It seemed that we had been enjoying ourselves far too much.

CHAPTER 3

My aunties

Our caretakers, whom we had to call Aunties, hated the work at Uptop and hated us. They often told us that if it wasn't for their love of our 'mother' they wouldn't be there.

The Aunties present at Uptop in the early years were Robina Carson, Ilene Johnson, Vera McLeod and Hazel Dalton. While these ladies were looking after us, life was not too bad. We received beltings and missed out on food, but their punishments were nothing like what was to come later. I remember being whacked on my backside with a purple slipper or a ruler. We were not hit too hard or an excessive number of times, although I think the discipline was tougher than young children should receive. Usually punishment was for something like bed-wetting or being naughty. Aunty Ilene was consistently good to us, and I remember her with a lot of fondness.

About 1976 Aunties Robina, Vera, Hazel and Ilene left. I remember being told something about Hazel betraying the cult – that she had told her husband about Uptop, or something similar. The Aunties were not supposed to reveal to anyone, not even their closest family, where they went for two weeks out of every four and what went on there. We were one of the major secrets in a cult completely dominated by secrecy. Everyone in the cult was expected to abide by the cult's motto of 'Unseen, Unheard,

My aunties 39

Unknown'. When Robina and the others left, Patricia Macfarlane, Elizabeth Whitaker, Wynn Belman and Margot MacLellan took over, marking the start of a new, considerably harsher regime. Helen Buchanan also started to come up during the week to give school lessons. And Uncle Leon Dawes came Uptop on weekends.

Anne Hamilton-Byrne believed in discipline absolutely. She was, we were told by the Aunties, Jesus Christ reincarnated. This was rarely explicitly said by her; usually she would just quote a saying of Jesus, such as 'I am the Way, the Truth and the Life', implying that it referred to her. Her religion was founded on distorted perceptions of the Hindu notion of 'karma': that you reap what you sow. Suffering as children was supposed not just to expiate the sins of this life, but also the sins of our past lives. Suffering built up our chances of salvation and redemption. It could therefore be said that Anne's religion practically called for child abuse.

Because she travelled so much, Anne left two books of instructions, referred to as 'Mummy's rule books'. These books listed penalties for infractions of rules. They had entries such as 'If David rocks or sways during meditation, he is to be hit over the head with a chair', and rules about everything – even about how many hours of piano practice each child was to do. These were signed by Anne and she encouraged the Aunties to belt us if we failed to comply.

I remember seeing her, when I was about 5 years old, holding up a little boy called Jerome, who was less than 2 at that time. She held him up by the ankles in front of the Aunties to 'show them the best way to belt a child'. He was being belted because he wet his bed. One of the adults' favourite sayings was 'You can't murder a bum, but you can always try'.

In Anne's absence the Aunties had control of us, and through 'Mummy's rule books' they enforced Anne's code of conduct. Liz Whitaker, in particular, had a cold, strange, scary personality. She was a horrible woman. Her constant snooping added to our feeling of being watched all the time. She would often listen to us talking among ourselves when we thought we were alone. She would climb under the house to listen to us talking after lights out, trying to catch us at something so she had an excuse to punish us. She would creep downstairs in an effort to catch us. Once she said she had taped a conversation we had in bed and would be sending it to Anne, who would be most displeased. It was supposed to be of us saying insubordinate things. That had us worried for a long time until we worked out that we hadn't actually said anything that night and she was just trying to trick us into a confession.

Aunty Liz was unpredictable and unstable – liable to go berserk with little or no provocation. Once Judith copped the full weight of her fury for not handing in a spelling test. Aunty Helen went upstairs to tell Liz about Judith's bad behaviour and Liz came roaring down wielding a metre ruler. She chased Judith into a corner between Stephen's bed and the pump-room door and laid into her with a vengeance. Judith was huddled on the floor trying to protect her head. Afterwards, her thigh was shockingly bruised.

I remember another incident that demonstrated Liz's temper, which occurred about 1982. It had been alleged that one of the boys had left the fan on overnight. Liz snatched up the metre ruler and started running around the room chasing the boys. She was wielding the ruler like a scimitar above her head, hitting anyone who came within range as hard as she could, with no regard for the damage. The boys were hit in the face and about the head. In the end Luke ran out of the room and locked the door. Aunty Liz started banging on it and screaming, completely enraged. Finally she calmed down, but a lot of the boys had been physically abused by her that day for no reason.

Trish Macfarlane seemed to particularly dislike me, although in some ways it was a love–hate relationship. I think she harboured a grudging respect for me as well. Despite the fact that she sometimes treated me with great cruelty and rage, I didn't mind Trish. It is a well-documented fact that prisoners can get to like their gaolers and I suppose that could have explained it.

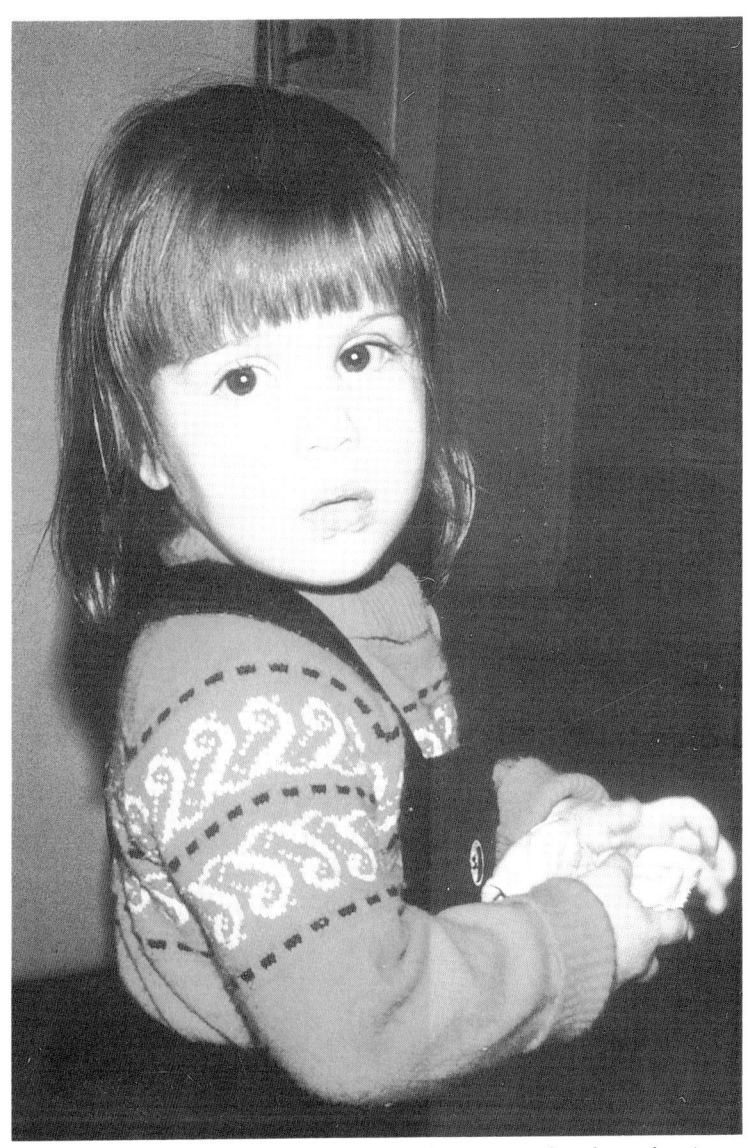

An ordinary childhood photo – except that I was already under Anne Hamilton-Byrne's control and living at Winberra, one of The Family's houses in the Dandenongs, Victoria.

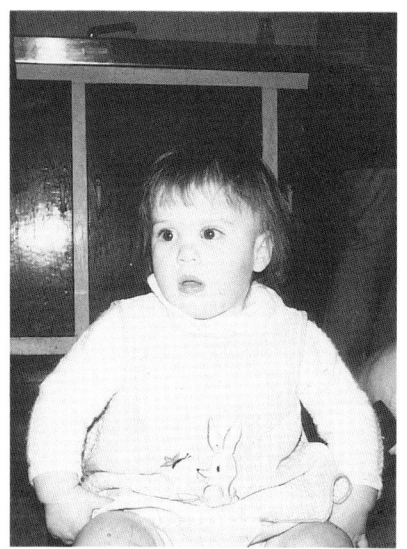

Sitting on the kitchen floor at Winberra as a 1-year-old.

All in a row: me and some of my 'brothers' and 'sisters' at Winberra, in about 1972. Left to right: Luke, me, Annette, Stephen, Anna and Timothy.

A sign at Kai Lama (Uptop), on Lake Eildon, warned off the curious. (Courtesy the Melbourne *Age*.)

A view of the house from the bottom yard. (Courtesy the Melbourne *Age*.)

All lined up in our best clothes for our baptism at St Mary's Catholic Church, in 1978. Left row, front to back: Julianne, Annette, Andrea, me, Arianne and Anna. Right row, front to back: Cassandra, David, Benjamin, Timothy, Luke, Stephen and John.

A special occasion: one of our rare Lake Eildon walks with Bill Hamilton-Byrne, in about 1982. Dinky-dog, on the left, sniffs the air, oblivious to the camera.

Sombre looks and special dresses for a photograph taken at Brook Farm, in England, in about 1980. Back row, left to right: Anna, Megan Dawes (Leon's daughter), me, Arianne and Susanne. Front row, left to right: Julianne, Judith and Annette.

The blue tracksuit phase, in about 1982. Back row, left to right: Anna and Arianne. Middle row, left to right: Luke, me and Timothy. Front row, left to right: Benjamin and Julianne.

Sitting on a plush velvet chair at Brook Farm.

Anne Hamilton-Byrne with her natural-born daughter, Natasha.

Anne posed as the loving mother with Anna for a photograph for The Family. By the 1970s, when it was taken, plastic surgery had radically altered Anne's appearance.

Portrait of the guru. The cult members were given this photo, and the bottom one of Anne and Anna on the opposite page, to put on their altars to worship.

Anne inscribed this photo of herself taken at Uptop: 'To Andrée [me], Love Mummy. We look alike they say you and I love'. Because Anne was in residence, there were baskets of fruit and the china tea service on display.

Anne's affection for her pets was not a pose.

The trappings of wealth: Anne in England in the mid-1980s.

Arianne and me with our beloved guru, Baba Muktananda. The photo was taken at the Hawaiian beach house in which he was staying in 1978.

Broom Farm, hidden behind snow-covered trees, in March 1987.

Anne's Catskill Mountains property is a forty-five-minute drive from New York City. There are three houses, one hidden by the two shown in the foreground. It was here that Anne and Bill were arrested in 1993, before their extradition to Australia.

This photo of cats at Broom Farm was inscribed 'All Family at Broom'. The dark structure in the background is the cattery.

My 'triplet brothers', Timothy (left) and Luke, at Brook Farm in 1985.

Anne inscribed this photo taken at Brook Farm in the 1980s as 'The lovely Summers day of the year 70 deg'. Left to right: Benjamin, Timothy, Bill, Luke, Anne and Cassandra.

Susanne, Anna and me in our 'Aquinel College' uniforms, during a school inspector's visit to Uptop in the 1980s.

Anna, captured behind the wire fence at Uptop by a roving photographer in August 1983. (Courtesy the Melbourne *Age*.)

Timothy and me at Broom Farm for Christmas 1986.

Actually, Aunty Trish was probably the most likeable person who looked after us. Although she could be very cruel, she was the only Aunty who ever let us have any fun, and now and then she even tried to make nice meals for us. Sometimes she would make pea soup for us and, as I said earlier, in later years she occasionally on a Friday let us pack up early after school to watch cricket on television or play outside. All this was unheard of, and against the rules, as was all fun and entertainment.

Trish spoke in a broad Australian accent and voted Labor. Anne decided her accent was deliberate and that she was flaunting her Australianness. This meant she was often in trouble with Anne because Anne affected an English accent and so it was obligatory for all of the other adults. We always got into trouble if we were caught using 'Australian', especially Australian slang; for example, 'yeah' instead of 'yes', or 'okay' instead of 'all right', was a punishable offence.

If Trish did not like a rule, she never pretended that she did, unlike all the others. I admired the way she would not change just because Anne wanted it, and the way she would sometimes ignore the rules. As I have said, she initiated and encouraged our interest in playing cricket, even though Anne thought the game was very rough and vulgar and banned it for long periods of time.

I think Trish was as much a victim of circumstances as we were. She had been in Anne's grip since her son died years before and Anne had pulled her from despair and guilt over his death. I think she hated being trapped Uptop for two weeks out of every four, and she let us know it. However, she should not have taken her frustration out on us. Although she didn't like looking after us 'brats', after a few days of sulking at the beginning of her fortnight – during which time she would be very hard on us – Aunty Trish gradually got better. We would usually look forward to her last week.

Aunties Margot, Wynn and Helen were junior to Liz and Trish and did not have the authority to give as many punishments. But they still had their moments. Margot was softer than the others at times, although she still gave out a lot of the less harsh beltings. Some of the children quite liked her.

Wynn, like Liz, was sneaky, and would gloat over us when we were being punished. She enjoyed making sarcastic remarks. She fancied herself as an interrogator and would be called upon whenever a confession was required for some misdeed, such as stealing vitamin C tablets. She shared Anne's obsession with diets and body shape and seemed to take sadistic pleasure in reducing our food intake and recording any subsequent weight loss. She made the smocks that we wore, and taught us some sewing.

Helen spent more time Uptop than any of the others. She was there every week, Monday to Friday, and functioned as our schoolteacher. She could be cruel and nasty, too, but generally she was a fairly decent sort. She could have her bad moods and take it out on us like the rest of them. Sometimes she was given the job of holding a kid down for the bigger beltings given by Trish and Liz; however, she was much less involved in hurting us than the others. Her favourite punishment was giving out lines when they were in common use.

Often we got the feeling that the Aunties hated us. It was all such a wretched chore to look after us. After all, they got nothing other than karmic merit for what they did. They sacrificed half their lives and, indeed, had to pay for the privilege of being Uptop. For it was their money that fed us – not Anne's.

The Aunties had to administer the complex set of rules outlined by Anne, live in the same Spartan conditions as us and comply with our rigid routine no matter what they felt like doing. They did have some perks, however – for instance they had bread and many other 'delicacies', which we did not. The food they ate we called 'Aunty food', and we often longed to be able to share it and tried to steal it.

The Aunties had to live with children they did not love or even like and who largely did not love or like them. All of them were financially strapped in the outside world, because they could only work part-time and because they were required, like all cult members, to give as much as one-third of their income to Anne. All of them made great sacrifices to look after us.

I only wish that the Aunties could have found it in their hearts to have loved us instead of resenting us. It was not our fault that we were all trapped in the same system. At least they had had at one time a choice about it, and could have left or refused to look after us if they had been brave enough. We didn't have any choice. As children we had no knowledge of or any opportunity to live any other way.

It seems to me that, in a way, the Aunties were, like us, victims of Anne. They did her bidding in every way. They left their families, they told no one about Uptop, they changed careers, they changed partners, they bore children and they abused children for her. All because that was what their Master wanted of them. Nevertheless the Aunties, as adults, chose to live that way so, in my view, must accept some responsibility for what happened to us.

Anne insisted that a lot of the women in the cult train as nurses, and we girls were all supposed to become nurses when we grew up. Medicine and nursing were part of the way she wanted the cult presented to the outside world: as a group of dedicated people doing good in the community. A cynic might say, of course, that it gave the cult access to drugs and to ill, vulnerable people who may have had money to leave behind when they died. Rumour has it that several old people died leaving their money to Anne or to one of her aliases or to one of the companies she controlled. No one knows exactly how some of these elderly people died; they were cremated immediately and their death certificates were signed by doctors who were members of the cult.

Training and working as nurses left women cult members with no time to look after their own families. Such women, prepared to give up their own families because of the word of the Master, were not about to quibble with 'Mummy's rule books' as applied to children not their own.

Several years ago, when I saw some of the Aunties in court on charges of defrauding social security, I felt sorry for them. They looked old and sad and harmless before the Bench, like people who had given a lifetime to something they did not really believe in. But then I reminded myself about the futility and the stupidity and the sheer brutality of our childhood and I no longer felt sorry for them. I was overwhelmed at that moment by intense anger. Had they ever taken pity on us?

Did the Aunties feel anything when we were beaten and cowering in terror in front of them? Did they feel bad when they saw we were so frightened of them that we couldn't even look at them for fear of punishment? Did they feel remorse when they saw us starving? No, they didn't care at all, or if they did they never showed it. They smirked at us and said that it was good for us.

How did they feel when they were half-drowning us in the punishment called 'ducking'? How did they feel when they saw the masses of bruises they had caused; when we were so miserable that we rocked and cried ourselves to sleep at night, crying out for our mummy and daddy to save us – for a mummy and daddy who were not there, who never heard? They felt no compassion for us then, never showed us any mercy.

Nor did they feel any sorrow when Stephen had repeated fits, his epilepsy sustained in the first place by the rough handling at Uptop. In about 1980, during a beating, Uncle Leon had thrown Stephen against a concrete shower recess with such force that he cracked his head. He was unconscious for many hours. A few days later he was taken down to Box Hill Hospital and X-rayed. A hairline fracture of the skull was discovered, which was to be the cause of his fits. Before the beating he was already congenitally blind and autistic. He did not need another handicap.

The Aunties showed no distress either when Judith pulled down her pants for yet another beating. They cared not at all that the whole of the upper thigh on her right leg was covered with a great mass of bruises because of one of Aunty Liz's uncontrollable rages.

Did the Aunties ever have doubts about their right to control us? I think they quickly stopped having any ordinary feelings of kindness and compassion once they started at Uptop. Or they learnt how to suppress them. Perhaps they were good mothers and kind nurses in the other two weeks of each month.

Despite my anger at that time, I now feel a lot less strongly about the Aunties. I now understand more about what was happening to them and what their motivation may have been. Anne had complete control of their lives. They had totally given over their will to her long before we were born. Most of them were not intrinsically evil people. They had merely subjugated all moral standards to the goal of obeying the Master's will.

Most of the Aunties felt they owed Anne their lives, for they believed that in times past she had helped them greatly to transcend huge personal problems. The debt they owed her because of this help justified undying and unquestioning devotion. It was too hard for them to challenge themselves about what they were doing because they were obeying the Master's orders, and to question anything connected with what she wanted was unthinkable. It was simply too threatening – better not to think and just to follow blindly.

Once the Aunties started to see incongruities or to have opinions about things, they may have wavered in their allegiance to Anne and that was a proposition too terrifying for them to contemplate, because a loss of faith would have meant punishment from a being who, in the Aunties' minds, was a reincarnation of God. Her wrath meant suffering far worse than death.

Today I don't feel any antipathy towards the Aunties. I don't want them to go to gaol and I don't even particularly want them to get into trouble for what they did to us. It was all Anne's fault, all by her design after all. These people only did what they were told. They were told to discipline us to within an inch of our lives and that is what they did.

CHAPTER 4

Suffer the little children

The guiding principle of our rigid existence at Uptop was discipline. Discipline was the word used to justify child abuse. It was discipline that we had to agree with no matter what.

Looking back I can see differences in the times and the ways we were punished. But always we were punished. Anne believed it was good for us. It fitted in with the karmic principles that the cult used to justify suffering and pain. Discipline was enforced in the early days with beltings and the deprivation of food. There were times when we were beaten almost every day, with hands or feet or anything the Aunties could find. As we got older and bigger it wasn't so easy for the Aunties to beat us and so they tried other methods of punishment, such as public humiliation, lines to write, the missing of 'privileges' and less common but more severe beltings.

Punishments came in waves. Whatever Anne considered the best way of disciplining us was enforced until she changed her mind. So I remember harsh times and softer times.

There was a particularly bad time, which lasted for about four years, between 1976 and 1980. During this period Anne and Bill were overseas most of the time, and there were a lot of foster children living with us. During these years we regularly suffered horrible beltings and missed one or two meals almost every day.

I was absolutely terrified of the Aunties a lot of the time when we were young and so were the others. I remember one morning we were downstairs on the concrete doing exercises supervised by Aunty Helen, when Trish called down saying that she wanted to see David K. She probably wanted to give him a belting because he'd wet his bed, which he did every night. But this morning David was so terrified when he heard her calling his name that he simply stood, rooted to the spot, and just lost control of his bowels. We all watched in horrified fascination as pieces of shit dropped out of his pants and onto the concrete, anticipating the terrible trouble he would be in now. Trish, very annoyed that he hadn't jumped to it, and interpreting his action as a new defiance, dragged him upstairs and gave him an even bigger belting than usual.

We were punished for not closing the lounge-room door, for dirtying our smocks, for not practising our piano pieces in the right order, for writing untidily, for not putting our shoes on fast enough, for making a mess, for talking when we were not supposed to, and for using forbidden words such as 'hate'. It didn't have to be much: make your bed wrongly; look at one of the Aunties with what was called 'dumb insolence' (quite what that was I never found out although I always wanted to ask – but that would have been insolence in itself); speak during Hatha yoga or lights out; or do a million other little things that infringed either the written laws, or the unwritten assumptions about the place of children in the scheme of things.

Megan Dawes was once denied meals for a day because she was caught wearing odd socks. We weren't allowed to go to the toilet until the designated recess time and so of course kids would wet their pants and be belted for that. One time we had a baby called Madeleine staying with us for a few weeks. She was locked in a cot all day with the sides up. She had not reached the walking stage and so couldn't get out of the cot to get to the toilet. However, that didn't stop the Aunties. Madeleine still got belted when she wet or dirtied her nappy. I remember Trish ordering me to bathe Madeleine in a basin after she had soiled herself. The water had to be icy cold as a punishment and Trish smacked her after I bathed her. She was screaming and I had difficulty holding her still in the cold water.

We were often punished for rocking. We used to rock ourselves to sleep at night because we felt so miserable, sitting up on our haunches and swaying to and fro, or just moving our head from side to side. Often after a belting we would call out 'Mummy, Daddy' as we rocked backwards and forwards, calling out to parents who were not there and did not care. When we were young, a few of us used to head bang as we rocked: it, too, was a way of seeking comfort. If we were caught, we received another belting, or we were put outside on the concrete for the remainder of the night or had cold water tipped over us. Rocking was considered to be bad because, even when we were tiny children it was interpreted as a form of sexual gratification.

On one of my visits to England, in 1976, Annette and I were punished by Anne for rocking by being locked in a dog kennel overnight. It was freezing cold weather, and although the kennel was large it also stank and had only a couple of dog blankets and urine-soaked straw on the floor. I remember trying to climb under the soggy straw in a desperate attempt to keep warm and how scared I was of being locked outside in the dark.

If we transgressed by word, thought or deed any one of the thousands of petty little rules that governed our lives, we were in trouble. There were so many rules that it was impossible to keep them all, and so many unfair reasons for punishment that, even when we tried our best, we still couldn't keep out of trouble.

I was often taken to the bathroom and made to bend over and bare my bottom to be hit with a stick. A silence would descend over the house when one of us was getting a belting. We were supposed to continue on with what we were doing and ignore it, but always a silence fell. We waited for the screams. We waited to hear the sounds of the beating, muffled by the bathroom door, the thuds, the pleading, the terror in the voices of our brothers and sisters.

One of my sisters had a theory about beltings: she maintained that we were only hit until the adults could hear us screaming. So she would start yelling the moment a belting began, or even before the adults had started! Many times I heard the Aunties say to her, 'Stop your screaming, we haven't even begun yet'. Maybe she was right. Certainly in the early years I would always break down and cry. I don't really know if it slowed them down or stopped them. How could I ever tell? I never actually timed a beating to see if my sister's theory worked.

As I got older I learnt to control myself. I remember deciding that, no matter how hard the Aunties hit me, I would not cry. It was pride – that dreadful thing Anne called ego. I thought crying meant you lacked honour and courage, so even with the most painful beltings, where you couldn't walk properly for days afterwards, I would try to hold out to the end. Because, I thought, if you cry you are broken, and I was not going to let them break me.

Soon I could often last a long belting without a single scream or tear. I was proud of that and perhaps that made things worse for me. I don't know. I only knew that after they had finished with me, after they had become exhausted from the effort it took to thrash me, they would send me off to bed and then and only then, in the privacy I found there, would I cry into my pillow. Even so, I tried to cry quietly. I didn't want them to know they had hurt me.

There were a few different kinds of beltings and lots of different 'tools'. The Aunties all had their favourite weapons. They would use anything they could find: bits of wood with nails and knobs, bamboo sticks (though these weren't much good because they tended to break), shoes, whips – basically anything handy that would hurt children. One of their worst instruments was the black three-cornered cane. It was made of reinforced plastic and so whichever way it hit you there was an edge against your flesh. It was a very painful thing, to be hit with that cane. It was hollow and made a whistling noise as it came down through the air.

The adults also used metre rulers to belt us. These were made from a plank of wood and they were a metre long and about 4 centimetres wide. Uncle Leon used these a lot. They were a bit heavy for most of the Aunties except Aunty Trish, who often used them. Perhaps she had stronger wrists than the others, and thus could wield them better.

Sometimes there were public beltings. During these we were all called up to the lounge-room and made to sit on the couch. The black stool was brought over and the offender had to lie over it and pull down his or her pants. The rest of us had to remain completely silent during a public belting. To murmur or cry or even look away was taken as a sign of insubordination, an expression of sympathy for the victim. This was considered a crime in itself, and anyone displaying such emotions was beaten as well.

So we watched steadfastly while our brothers and sisters clung to the stool and were thrashed. We watched as the black three-cornered cane come down against their skin again and again; we saw the welts rise. We watched them trying to stifle their sobs, trying to be brave. And then, almost inevitably, we watched them break down, howling and screaming for mercy.

I remember some of my worst beltings only because they were unjust. The ones I deserved, according to our perverted sense of justice, I usually forgot pretty quickly. Anyway it wouldn't be possible to remember every belting I had because for a while, it seemed, the rule was 'A belting a day keeps evil away'. When the adults were deciding on punishments for us, they used to laugh and repeat their joke about not being able to murder a bum.

When I was only 6 or 7 years old, I was dragged in front of the household assembly by Anne and publicly scorned and humiliated for being a 'goody-goody'. It was probably true at the time. At that stage I was trying to keep out of people's way. A few of the others were also trying to keep a low profile. But we even got into trouble for being too good. After that I gave up on such a policy, and whatever mischief was going on I'd be involved in it. And, in time, I began to be seen as a ring-leader. With Anna and Luke, I was always one of the first suspects in any trouble.

When someone had done something wrong, the adults would hold interrogation sessions. Leon Dawes told us that he had been a member of the Criminal Investigation Bureau, and he used to fancy himself as an expert at extricating confessions from the guilty, namely us. If, for example, some food had been stolen but no one was owning up, we would be called upstairs one at a time and made to sit on a chair. A light would be shone in our faces and Leon would say things like, 'You might as well make things easier on yourself and tell me all about it now, because we know you did it'. He would try to trick us into a confession by pretending he already knew everything from his prior questioning of the others. In retrospect, it was like a scene from a bad B-grade film, but at the time it was quite terrifying, especially for the younger ones facing on their own this person with seemingly omnipotent powers. The younger ones would break down quite easily and tell him everything they could think of. I used to try to brazen it out and not say anything because the more you told him the more he'd try to trick you into saying something that contradicted your previous story.

When I was about 10, we were told by Anne that we were going to have a 'round table conference' for the entire household at which everyone would be allowed to air his or her views. I suppose I should have realised beforehand what kind of a session it was going to be – a total farce of democracy – but I didn't. I was excited by the idea that we might get a chance to complain about the system, and stupidly thought the meeting meant that Anne wanted to listen to our views. Instead it turned into a dobbing session for the Aunties. Luke was reported to Anne for climbing over the yard fence to get a ball and he then received a 'light' punishment – about twenty belts to his bare backside with Anne's heeled shoe.

After belting Luke, Anne asked if any of us wanted to speak. I was silly enough to make a comment. I forget what I complained about but it offended Anne because she started hitting me about the head with her hand and her shoe, yelling that I was impertinent. Then she chased me to the girls' room and hit me with a broom that had been left propped up in the hallway. She seemed out of control. She was using the head of the broom and the wood was digging into me. I thought then, as I often did during a bad belting, that she would kill me, and that it would only be if she took mercy on me that I would be spared. I never knew when a beating would end. I didn't know then – none of us did – that there was an outside world that could have stopped her killing us.

Despite the attempts to make us inform on our brothers and sisters, as I grew older I tried to live by certain principles. I believed in a kind of code of 'honour among thieves'; that it was cowardly to inform on others, even though the adults tried to get us to spy on each other and dob in anyone we suspected of planning mischief. I thought dobbing was as low as someone could get, and I tried to make it a rule that I would not dob, no matter how bad things got. I used to be disgusted with those who did. Some of the children would blurt out anything as soon as it looked like the Aunties might be organising an inquisition.

I couldn't stand those who were too scared to do anything but creep around like little mice telling on everyone, and especially on me it seemed, to curry favour with the Aunties; those who could never face a punishment on their own without turning in the kids who'd been in on it with them. I thought that these children were pathetic and spineless at the time. Still, it was understandable behaviour when you consider the sick little world we lived in.

Probably the smartest thing would have been to sit tight and try to remain unnoticed. If anyone was noticed he or she paid for it. And the fear of being punished was so great, so all-consuming, that many would do anything to avoid it. Being punished alone was even worse because then you were reviled by everyone – the other kids as well as the adults. Much better to have company for a punishment. At least then there was someone to share the misery and the brutality.

Although I thought it was cowardly to inform on the others, I once did something far worse than that. That is a time I will remember forever with guilt and shame. My failure to take the blame for something I had done caused the first ever 'ducking' in the household. That experience of terror, in fact of fear for our lives, came about all because of my cowardice.

Ducking was something dreamed up by Anne in about 1979. She thought she needed to devise some new laws to stop our dreadful 'lying, sneaky, sinful' ways. She said to us 'You are all thieves, sneaks and liars'. She decided that the Aunties would put our heads into buckets of water, again and again, until we confessed to whatever crime we were meant to have done. Anne said to the Aunties that it was 'better to be drowned (or better to be dead) than to be a liar'.

Because of our constant hunger, we had developed a bartering system, a kind of blackmarket where anything could be swapped for food. For instance one biscuit was worth two big apples, or three small ones, or ten vitamin Cs, or a handful of raisins; it all depended on the rarity of the currency.

One morning during my piano practice one of the foster girls came in and we decided to steal some vitamin C tablets. (When we were little we were given massive doses of vitamins and the dishes were lined up on a bench before the meal and covered with tea-towels.) We sneaked into the kitchen and stole about thirty vitamin C tablets from the dishes on the kitchen bench. Vitamin Cs were orange flavoured and were the nearest thing we got to lollies. They were hot property on our blackmarket and were some consolation for going for days without food. At least they helped clear away the taste of stale vomit in your mouth. So they were often saved from our meals illegally, and then swapped.

On this occasion our theft was discovered at lunchtime: half the dishes were missing their vitamin C tablets. The Aunty who did the dishes insisted she had not made a mistake. That left but one option: they had been stolen. The Aunties decided that it was time to apply Anne's new law.

Aunty Liz came to us before lunch and said that if someone

didn't own up in the next five minutes there would be a ducking. I should have stepped forward then and there and saved everyone. Usually I could do it, but not this time. I don't know why; for once my fear seemed to paralyse me. I literally couldn't make myself take the step to stop this nightmare craziness. When Aunty Liz asked me, 'Did you do it?', all I could do was shake my head. I was sick with fear. Then it seemed things were going so fast that I had no chance to say anything. It was all out of my control.

We were lined up in two rows, boys in one, girls in the other, and told to pull down our pants and bend over. Aunty Liz went along the row with the black three-cornered cane and belted each of us. Of course, she had a fairly good idea of who was responsible, so I got the hardest and longest beating.

Then we were sent downstairs to wait in our rooms while the Aunties filled the buckets. A bucket was placed on the bench outside the back door, the idea being that the Aunties would force us to kneel down on the concrete one by one and then two or three of them would immerse our heads in the bucket. At least one Aunty would be needed to steady the bucket and hold our hands behind our backs, and another would be required to keep our heads under.

We were dragged out one by one, kicking and screaming. The boys were first and one of the worst parts was hearing their howls of terror and anger, followed by the gurgling when they went under, and then their strangled, gasping screams as their heads emerged intermittently from the water. We listened to the utter silence while they were under the water and the thumps as they were thrown away. Finally we heard the exhausted, hopeless sobbing of each discarded child.

Some of the kids fought. I wasn't one of them; I just took the biggest breath I could each time they let me up and resigned myself to my fate.

That was our first ducking and it was pure terror. I remember the feeling that went through the house. I can feel it now. We believed the Aunties could kill us because we had been so bad. We didn't know that it was illegal to punish us as they did, let alone to kill us. We didn't know there was a society out there that could stop them; that there were any rules apart from theirs. To us they had complete control over life and death.

I cannot describe that feeling of knowing that you are completely powerless, of thinking that you could be killed at any moment. Once Megan and I hid in the cupboard, holding hands tightly to give each other strength. We children asked ourselves in anguish again and again, 'Where is our mummy to save us from this?'. We thought that if she only knew how much we were suffering under this new rule she would stop it. How little we knew.

The next time we got ducked was when Aunty Lillibet's violin rest went missing. She said one of us had stolen it and so we were to be belted and ducked until a child confessed. Aunty Liz did the ducking again. Some of the girls got out of it because Jerome, out of sheer terror, said he had taken it. He was treated even worse after he admitted to the crime. It turned out that Lillibet had just temporarily misplaced her violin rest. A few weeks later she found it where she had left it, in her house in Melbourne. There were no apologies. But then there never were.

There weren't many duckings Uptop. There didn't need to be. The fear the mere word evoked was usually enough to have us do zombie-like whatever they wanted. We would do almost anything to avoid a ducking: the threat turned child against child. The house would be reduced to a cave of terror.

As I said, I remember the unjust punishments more than the ones I thought I deserved. The time I was almost ducked for the third time was one of those. I was dragged by my hair by Aunty Trish and Aunty Wynn to the bath, which had been filled with water, but for some reason Anna was able to save me. Anna became hysterical, screaming 'Don't kill my sister, don't kill my sister', and somehow, on that day, it stopped them. God knows why, because the distress of the other children had never swayed them from continuing a punishment before. The Plasticine under a doll had gone missing and I was the prime suspect – simply because I was already in trouble that day – though I had nothing to do with the missing Plasticine. The incident was just further evidence of the utter randomness of punishments. Punishment was often about being in the wrong place at the wrong time.

Strangely enough, although Anna saved me from a ducking, it was also because of her that I got one of my worst beltings – on the same day.

Anne sometimes used to give us silly little china figurines and trinkets, the only 'playthings' she ever bought for us children. She would spread them out on her bed and we would be lined up to look at them, before being ordered to return them to their boxes. We were not allowed to touch them without permission and we certainly could not play with them – they were, in fact, very inappropriate presents for children, but that never occurred to Anne. Against all the rules, the little china figurines were sometimes swapped – those who didn't have food to swap on the blackmarket would swap anything of value and, as you can probably guess, all of this was strictly forbidden. (Cassandra lost practically her whole Garfield collection in this way until we older ones intervened. She had been sent the collection by a friend of Anne's in England.)

I was often called in to mediate in alleged rip-offs. After kids had devoured the food they would often regret losing their treasure or being so much in debt. Whether I intervened often depended on who the victim was. I would always help Cassandra because she was so starved, but with some of the others I took the view that it was pure greed that had lost them their belongings, and that a deal was a deal and no one should wimp out.

Sometimes misunderstandings would also result from swaps. The wrong things would end up in the wrong drawers and it would cause a big ruckus if the adults found out. That was how I ended up in trouble on this particular day. I was discovered with some china belonging to Anna in my drawer. I know some of the kids still think I stole Anna's things but I'm sure I didn't. I think I was framed. It was considered a very serious crime and, after my near ducking for supposedly stealing the Plasticine, we were all sent to bed without any tea and ordered to wait for my big punishment the next morning.

I didn't sleep much that night. I tossed and turned and thought about what the Aunties might have in mind for me. I found out I was to have a public belting and then to stay in bed all weekend without any food, receiving periodic beltings. Also, no one was to be allowed to speak to me.

I remember the belting well. The kids were having brunch when I was called upstairs, and everyone was forced to watch my punishment. The black stool, which was about a metre high, was placed in the middle of the lounge-room floor. I was told to pull down my pants and bend over. Actually, that was one of the worst things about beltings: pulling your pants down was so ignominious, as was bending over that stupid black stool. The pain was one thing, but the shame was worse.

Aunty Trish had her usual weapon – the black three-cornered cane. I didn't want to bend over in front of everyone so by the end of the belting I was practically naked because every time she grabbed my clothes I struggled and pieces of clothing kept coming off. The belting seemed to go on forever and I was burning with embarrassment because I didn't have many clothes left on.

Then I was kicked downstairs to bed again. On the second day I sat up and vomited all over the bed, which at least caused a bit of a diversion because I was then allowed to change the sheets and go to the bathroom. Apart from that I had to stay in bed the whole time. Bill came in on Sunday and I'd been looking forward to that because I thought he might let me off. But no, he just gave me a lecture on my sins and left, thankfully without delivering another belting as I had been promised.

The only good part of that weekend was Anna. She did something I'll never forget – she smuggled me in a biscuit from her own brunch. If she'd been caught she'd have been in almost as much trouble as I was. An act of such kindness was so rare Uptop, it stands out still and I will always be touched by her giving me that biscuit.

Survival was usually an individual matter, a case of every person for himself or herself, although sometimes on someone's birthday a few of us might gang together and give the particular person a few pieces of fruit we'd saved. But not many kids would risk so much to go against the system and although Anna's biscuit didn't stop my hunger – for by then I'd been without food for days – it lifted my heart just a little.

Another memorable belting I received was when I was about 12 years old. Annette and I had worked out a bartering system for fruit because she preferred oranges and I preferred apples. To the left of my place at the table was a large telescope with a bag over it. Annette and I would each place the piece of fruit we were going to swap in the telescope and then, later on, when we had the chance, such as while we were on the way to a piano lesson, we would take the other piece of fruit. There was also a small bin in the centre of each table for fruit peelings. As well as the fruit swapping I went through a stage of wrapping up all my vitamins, except the lolly-like vitamin C, with my fruit peelings and dropping them in the bin. I'd been carrying out these activities for a couple of weeks when Aunty Liz decided she was onto me.

She walked down the room to the fireplace and waited until I emptied the tablets into the bin then came straight back, looked into the bin and said 'What have we here?'. Next she walked over to the telescope and took out the fruit Annette and I had been hiding. Doubly incriminated, I was sent downstairs and interrogated about Annette's involvement.

Liz went into a rage. I had to bend over Susanne's bed in the girls' room and I remember that the curtains were open and hoping that no one was looking in. I had my pants pulled down around my ankles and Liz was using a round stick, a bit less than a metre long and about 2 centimetres wide. She hit me forty to fifty times. At first I was determined to be brave, but it got too much for me and I was crying hard and begging her to stop. She hit me on my backside, my back and my legs until she was too tired to hit me any more. Next day I had bruises all over me.

When Liz was exhausted she sent me to bed. Annette was then brought down for her punishment. She was already crying, even though she kept denying the whole thing. I screamed at Liz to give me another belting because Annette had had nothing to do with it. She was becoming hysterical so I took pity on her. I was very worried about Annette because she was in such a state. In the end Annette didn't get her belting and I didn't get another one. A small victory!

I remember a couple of the more bizarre punishments quite clearly. I saw Anne put David K.'s hand in a fire burning in the big stone fireplace at Uptop – a fire was usually only lit if Anne was there. David had thrown a green plastic frog in the fire, and that's why Anne burnt his hand. Liz Whitaker helped Anne hold his hand in the fire. I don't remember how long they held it there but he was screaming and struggling. The rule Uptop was, if you played with fire, you got your hand burnt in the fire.

A similar thing happened to me when I was 9 or 10 years old. I was fooling around with a candle we had placed on a table. I don't know why we had lit candles that night; maybe the power was out. I began showing off, passing my fingers through the flame really fast. Anne caught me doing it and held my index and third fingers over the flame. I don't think it was for very long because I was struggling, but it was extremely painful. I remember looking at the blisters after I was sent to bed. Julieanne also got her hand burnt for some trivial reason.

Another strange punishment of Anne's was to wash our mouths out with soap occasionally if we were cheeky. She would take individual culprits into the bathroom, belt them, push them under the cold shower, drag them out by the hair and attempt to stuff a cake of Velvet soap into their mouths. If this did not result in the soap being swallowed, the victims were made to stand there and eat it.

When I was little Anne used sometimes to slam a carving knife down on the bench while we were eating and scream at us that the next person to step out of line, or move, or be caught with bad manners, would get their 'bum cut off'. It was a prospect that filled us with terror, though it was just a ploy to keep us scared and under control.

For a short period Anne tried to control us by instituting a house system similar to the systems some schools use. It fizzled out in less than a year. We were divided into two houses, one called Andromeda, one called Universe. The idea was that, as well as our usual punishments, we lost points for disobedience, for being poor at schoolwork, for impertinence or for breaking any of the rules. It was supposed to be a tragedy if you lost points because one house was supposed to beat the other and then get prizes. Of course this never eventuated. There was an even spread of boys and girls in the houses. Boys were generally at a disadvantage because they always lost points. The house with David K. lost five points every morning because of his bed-wetting.

Because we had little or no spare time, writing lines became one of the more annoying and invasive punishments that Anne devised. Our first batch of lines was for wearing nail-polish. One time, in about 1980, when Susanne went down to visit Natasha (who was supposed to be her mother) she was given some make-up, which she brought back with her. A few days later some of us were experimenting with it and put on some of the nail-polish.

Of course we could not conceal the evidence of our mischief, and we never would have done it if we could have predicted Anne's reaction when she found out. She screamed abuse at us on the phone, calling us sluts and whores and accusing us of one of the most serious and indefensible crimes: that of thinking about sex. She had dreamed up a new punishment for this heinous crime: 5000 lines each. We had to write 'We must never again use nail-polish or put make-up on ourselves without permission'.

We weren't supposed to eat again until we had finished this first batch. But I don't think Anne realised just how long 5000 lines would take to write. It took at least a week to complete that many because we were only allowed to write them during our breaks, not during schooltime or time allotted to spiritual things. It took so long to write them with these constraints that eventually Anne had to back away from her threat that we weren't to eat until we had finished. We would have been dead pretty soon otherwise. Actually that first time we got lines was the only time I remember Aunty Liz ever doing anything decent for us. She was so worried after we had missed three or four days' meals, with still no end to the line writing in sight, that she rang Anne and asked if we could be fed. Anne said 'No', and although Liz could not disobey her she 'accidentally' left the fruit store under the house unlocked. She knew that we would raid it and we did, but for once she turned a blind eye.

After that we got lines for anything. It now seems laughable. I once got 5000 for questioning whether Christabel Wallace was a senior Aunty. Because Christabel was offended by this impertinence I had to write out 5000 times 'Aunty Christabel is a Senior, Senior Aunty'. Another time I had a backlog of 22 000 lines to write. It seemed that they would never end, that I would never have free time again. However, soon I could write quite fast, and was always the first to finish a batch. I used to sit up with some of the others at night in the cupboard in the girls' room with a candle we had pinched. It is ironic that stealing a candle was in itself a crime that was worth a punishment far more serious than a few thousand lines.

The Aunties told us that they had a computer that would count the lines so we had to do the exact number required. More fool me. Not knowing what a computer was, I believed them and so for years would laboriously count the lines and write the exact number at the end of each page.

Writing lines had its funny side because there were certain lines that were guaranteed to be given out again and again, certainly to me. One of them was 'I must not be impertinent to my elders'. So when I had some extra time I'd write a few thousand extra, or steal back some of the batches I had already written and stash them under my mattress for later use. Cheating at lines was of course forbidden and I would have been in dire strife had I been caught at this.

If we were caught writing the words in columns, such as 'I, I, I, I . . . must, must, must, must . . . ', to do the work faster – instead of writing out the full sentence each time – the whole lot would be torn up and we would have to start all over again. Still, lines were not as bad as beltings.

The punishments were so extreme and out of proportion to the supposed misdeed that it was hard to make any sense of them. Once I was caught stomping up the stairs when told to do piano practice instead of the more enjoyable biology. At about the same time, Andrea had committed the offence of reminding Natasha of one of Anne's own rules.

My moodiness and Andrea's show of impertinence were taken by Anne to be indicative of excessive ego (one of the worst crimes of which you could be accused and, again, one against which there was no defence). She prescribed the following punishments: our food was to be reduced; there were to be no piano or biology lessons or reading for pleasure; we were to be shunned by the other children; our meagre access to television was to be reduced to nothing; we were not to meet visiting cult members; we were to be excluded from any treat the others were granted; I was to sleep on the floor in the bathroom one week, Andrea the next; we were to be excommunicated by Anne and Bill and ignored in their letters and phone calls apart from occasional abuse and snide comments; and Andrea and I, who were best friends, were to be kept apart – no doing schoolwork in the same room, no talking, no sleeping together. Some of these punishments, including our separation, continued for twelve months; the majority for six – six to twelve long months under the watchful eyes of the Aunties and the other children, who had been forced into the role of warders.

Anne's brutality is well illustrated by an incident that involved Julieanne. Julieanne had been cheeky to Aunty Liz one morning. Later, when Anne made one of her regular phone calls, Liz told Anne of Julieanne's 'impertinence'. When it was my turn to speak to Anne on the phone, Anne instructed me to tell Aunty Liz to bring Julieanne upstairs and place her beside the phone. Liz brought Julieanne upstairs and forced her onto the bed.

Anne then said to me, 'Tell Elizabeth to belt Julieanne'.

I hesitated. Anne immediately picked up on this and ordered me to say it to Liz. 'I want you to tell her this: to belt Julieanne and make sure it's a good one [belting] because I want you to hold up the phone so I can hear the screams. It has to be good enough to hear screams.'

I may have talked Anne out of it because I don't remember witnessing the belting, but I can't forget her words. I can never forget those words. They haunt me and remind me of how bad things were whenever I forget for a moment just how cruel life was up there.

When I was young I hated myself. I don't think I was unusual among the kids; I think we all hated ourselves for we had learnt well the lesson that children were inherently evil.

We all used to hurt ourselves deliberately. If the adults weren't hurting us we would do it ourselves. We would all stand along the bathroom railing doing a valsalva manoeuvre, which involves holding your breath really hard and tensing up all your muscles until you go black in the face, faint and fall over. It became a sort of macabre competition to see who could last the longest. I don't know why we did that: we just did it.

We couldn't reveal our emotions or let off steam by becoming angry or having an argument or a tantrum because that was forbidden. The only power we had was to turn our hurt on ourselves. Kids would do things like pour cold water over themselves, and some would pick a sore until it got badly infected. I often used to burn myself or prick my arms with pins or scissors rubbed in dirt. I still have little scars all over my arms because of that practice.

I often fantasised about killing myself, by drowning in the lake or poisoning myself with Dettol. It was only later, after we had escaped from the cult, that I found out that many of the others had similar delusions.

At puberty my self-hatred grew worse. When my breasts started to develop I thought that it was proof that all Anne had said about me being fat and ugly was true; all that she had said about my dirty mind was right and manifested in what was happening to me. I was actually turning into some sort of sexual beast. I wanted to bind up my breasts. I envisaged cutting them off, but the thought of the blood finally stopped me. I would pray at night for God to make my breasts go away but, as usual, he took no notice of my pleas.

Why did we hate ourselves so much even when we were only little kids? I think it was because we had been so successfully indoctrinated with the idea that we were inherently unworthy. If you are told incessantly that you are horrible, that you are ugly, fat, evil, stupid and inferior, you start to believe it. As a child you know no other truth than that which you are taught by those around you.

Perhaps, too, we wanted to hurt ourselves because it didn't feel right unless we were being punished for something. It somehow felt better when we were hurting. In a strange sort of way that offered comfort. Maybe it was because the only form of human contact we knew was physical abuse. Even if it hurt it was interaction and attention and human touch: all the things that children need and crave.

CHAPTER 5

The hungry years

For most of my early childhood, I was constantly hungry. We were starving and it was Anne's policy that we should remain so. We were so hungry we ate dirt and leaves. We were so hungry we ate grass and scavenged in the rubbish bins. We were so hungry we ate the food put out for the cats and dogs and we ate the bread and seed left for the birds. We were so hungry we stole anything we could. Vitamin C tablets were considered manna from Heaven.

The obvious reason for our constant hunger was the frugal diet. But there was another reason that was equally to blame. Deprivation of food, or 'missing meals', was a favoured punishment. When we were made to miss meals for a few days, we would often vomit on the second or third day. Some would vomit by the evening of the first day. We were made to continue with our ordinary routine, even though by the second or third day we were very weak. If we acted in a pathetic manner because we felt weak, the Aunties punished us for malingering or they would say that we were just trying to get sympathy from the other children. Even though we might vomit during Hatha yoga, we were shown no sympathy.

The Aunties, especially Liz Whitaker, had been known to poke through the vomit to make sure we hadn't eaten any food we had saved or stolen. By the second day I usually just vomited bile, but they still looked through it. If any evidence of food was found we would be punished even more severely.

Occasionally Anne would introduce fad diets for the adult cult members. A grape diet or an apple diet might be decreed and maintained for a few weeks. She also put a lot of members on the Pritikin diet. However, she never seemed to follow these stringent diets herself.

The years between 1976 and 1980, when I was about 6 to 10 years old, were the years when this punishment by starvation was mostly practised. It was not unusual for meals to be denied for up to three days for the most trivial of offences. There were many rules: it was impossible to know them all, and we often only found out that we had broken one when we got punished for it. If we squeezed the toothpaste tube too hard or in the wrong way or didn't put the lid back on it, we were punished; if we got our smocks dirty or expressed 'dumb insolence', we were punished by starvation.

The irony was that stealing food was the crime for which we were most often punished. It was a Catch-22 situation: we were so hungry from missing meals that we stole food, but when we stole food we were made to miss more meals. It wasn't surprising that most of us were obsessed with food.

Extraordinary measures were taken to prevent us from stealing food. The kitchen cupboards were padlocked. There was a chain and padlock around the fridge, and an Aunty was delegated to guard the kitchen at all times. Amazingly, despite these measures, we were sometimes successful. But, more often than not, the ever-vigilant Aunties noticed immediately if anything was missing. If we were lucky we'd be caught after we had devoured the booty, because it would fortify us for our usual punishment: further missed meals. There would also be an obligatory belting and then would come the report to Anne, which meant taunts from her and more threats.

As well as trying to steal, we used to scavenge for what we

could. The younger children would crawl under the dining table after meals, supposedly to sweep up any mess, but really to gather up and eat whatever scraps or crumbs had fallen. Others of us would raid the rubbish bins and the compost bin. I only ate leaves and grass to assuage the dreadful emptiness in my stomach. It was a desperation measure. Any edible plants and flowers were dealt with very quickly. I remember the nasturtiums in particular disappeared within minutes of flowering. We also ate the honeysuckle bush, and a type of grass that had a sweet-tasting centre. There was a rumour that one of the kids used to eat his own faeces. According to some, he also used to smear them on the toilet wall, but I never saw him doing that.

The stale and mouldy bread that the Aunties put out for the birds was highly prized. There was a bird platform protruding from the verandah and bits of bread and birdseed would drop from the platform onto the ground. We would slink around in the bottom yard waiting for the moment when the Aunties would put out the bread, waiting for any crumbs that might inadvertently fall from the platform or be dropped by the birds. Once Jerome was caught eating the birdseed and he was made to eat birdseed for a day instead of his ordinary meals.

At one stage, when the Aunties were regularly making us miss meals for several days at a time, Leon Dawes became concerned. We were getting so skinny he thought we looked like concentration camp victims so he spoke to Anne about it. It was after that that we started getting brunch on weekends, and the punishment of starvation for long periods of time became much rarer.

Often the food that we did get would not be very palatable. Despite all the cats, there were innumerable mice in the house and frequently the muesli we were given on the weekend would contain mouse-shit. We were not allowed to complain about this: we were simply told to pick it out, although many ate it instead for nourishment. Only once do I remember there being a mass refusal to eat the food Uptop. This act of defiance was brought on by Annabelle, one of the cats. She used to sleep on the top of the fridge and get high on the gas she inhaled. She was extremely fat and lazy, and rather than use up her energy by making her way outside when nature called, she would often simply urinate down the back of the fridge. Occasionally she would stagger down onto the bench and relieve herself there. One Saturday she urinated into a pot of porridge that was intended for us children. For some reason we were not given the porridge that day so it was heated up the next morning for brunch. A strong stench emanated from the pot and filled the house. We guessed what had happened, and when the porridge was served we wordlessly as one got up from the table and put our bowls on the bench in protest. Everyone except Stephen. We later joked that he wolfed the porridge down so fast he never even knew what he was eating. Aunty Liz claimed that we were imagining that the porridge had cat urine in it, but she was not game to taste it in front of us, and eventually gave us some bran instead. This was one of the only battles we ever won; generally we were not in any position to be picky about our food.

When I was about 11 years old, Annette and I discovered a wonderful thing: toast! We found that if we snuck out at night-time we could get into one of the caravans that some of the Aunties used to sleep in and make ourselves toast and Vegemite. We chose nights when we knew they were not there, of course, and we were never actually caught in the act. We loved these little feasts but, like all good things, they came to an end. One night I wiped a dirty knife on a tea-towel and left behind a smear of Vegemite. Aunty Liz found the tea-towel and when Anne came Uptop the following Friday we were called together for a pow-wow.

I wasn't going to own up at first, because I was convinced that there was really no evidence to suggest that the crime had been committed. However, Anne threatened to get Kerry Kulkens, a famous witch from the Dandenong area and supposedly a friend of hers, to look into her crystal ball to identify the hand of the culprit. Anne said that if the guilty person did not confess, Kerry

Kulkens would cast a spell to make something 'very horrible go wrong with them'. This threat scared me considerably and I confessed straight away.

As punishment Anne belted me in front of everyone with her shoe, kicked me downstairs and threw a chair after me. Although this wasn't the worst beating I'd ever had and I knew I'd done the wrong thing and been caught, I nevertheless felt very sorry for myself afterwards. I was upset because at the time it seemed like the last straw, that I could never hope to be good enough to live up to Anne's expectations. That evening these thoughts of unworthiness and failure so overwhelmed me that I thought I'd run away. In the naive way of children I thought I'd go and hide in the bush. I knew for certain that once I had left Uptop I would be in such trouble I would never be able to return. I think I thought I'd live alone in the bush like Robinson Crusoe or the Swiss Family Robinson. I had some fancy idea of going up to Fraser National Park and surviving in the wild, like the heroes I had read about in books.

After we all went to bed I waited until the others were asleep. I put pillows in my bed to make it look as if I were still there and I tried to get some jumpers to take with me, but I accidentally woke Annette. I told her I was running away and not to tell anyone. In a little bag I packed two apples I'd been saving, a jumper and my teddy bear, and I left.

I got outside the property without incident and then I didn't know what to do, so I just kept on walking. Actually, although it was dark and I was all alone, I was a bit excited by the idea of being free. I was also terrified about being murdered so I decided I would have to be very careful and stay away from people. After a while I got tired and lay down to sleep beside a log. When I woke up I wanted to go to the toilet but I didn't have any toilet paper. It was cold and raining a little. I didn't think anyone Uptop would look for me, but afterwards Anne told me that everyone had been frantic.

Eventually I found myself drifting back towards Uptop, in spite of the terror I felt at the thought of the punishments I would receive. I never considered contacting any outside person and if I'd seen a stranger I'd have hidden. I have to admit, being on my own in the bush was not what I'd expected. I did not have the first idea of how to survive outside Uptop. I had never been anywhere on my own before, never been outside the confines of the property on my own, never had to fend for myself or undertake any activity that had not been prescribed by adults. I also had no one to whom I could turn.

My return to Uptop was not what I had imagined either. I had scarcely been away for twenty-four hours yet instead of punishing me with more beltings and abuse, Anne showered me with affection and attention. This was extremely perplexing at the time. Whereas in the past I'd thought she'd hated me, now she was sending me downstairs to have a hot shower and be given toast. I was very aware of the bizarre contradiction: the day before I had been beaten for daring to take some toast and now I was being rewarded with the same food for running away. It was very confusing. I didn't understand why I was being treated so well. I'd expected terrible punishment and retribution, but here was Anne telling me how worried she had been about me. I found it almost unbelievable because I had been so convinced that she hated me and I had run away because my life was so miserable without her love.

After this episode my status seemed to change, and with it my perception of myself. Before I had felt like a nobody because I did not think Anne had noticed my existence. Now she started to treat me as if she loved me and had noticed me for the first time — I think she was impressed that I had the guts to run away. I felt special because I had found out now that Anne loved me, and I became devoted to her. But loving Anne Hamilton-Byrne was full of confusion: I could never understand her.

If we were often denied food, the opposite was true of drugs. Anne fancied herself as a healer and we were subjected to the same drug-taking practices as the adult members of The Family. She ordered huge amounts of medication for us. Most of the drugs the Aunties administered accordingly were unprescribed, but others had been prescribed by the doctors in the cult for adult cult members. I know now how dangerous and inappropriate for children they were.

Anna was given Tegretol, a prescription anti-convulsant drug for epilepsy, supposedly to cure her of her temper tantrums. It was more likely to have been administered for its sedative side-effects. The Aunties gave it to her three times a day. Anne ordered this drug and Doctor Christabel Wallace, a prominent cult member, apparently compliantly prescribed it. This doctor still practises as a general practitioner in Bayswater North.

We regularly received major tranquillisers such as Anatensol and Serepax. We were all given the benzodiazepines Valium and Mogadon on a daily basis. Apart from the sheer monotony of our daily lives, I blame the large doses of tranquillisers I received as a child for my inability to remember any significant dates. Large portions of my past are blurred, the chronology is unclear, and I experience none of the vividness most people associate with childhood memories.

We would be given extra Mogadon if the adults thought we needed calming down. The Aunties would say, 'Have a Moggy, you're feeling upset'. We were also given Largactil, Stelazine and Tofranil. Often our food tasted strange and sometimes we would uncover little tablet pieces or powder in it. When we asked about these findings, the Aunties would say, 'It's just something to calm you down'.

The climax of each child's drug taking came in the cult practice known as 'going-through'. I describe my own experience of this later in the book. During the process, also know as 'clearing', we were given LSD and a number of other hallucinogenic drugs. Going-through was basically a sustained LSD trip. It was meant to 'clear' our souls and take us to a higher plane of understanding. It was possibly also the key to Anne's spiritual influence over us.

I had my first going-through at 14 and afterwards I was given Largactil, haloperidol and Valium by Anne to 'slow me down'. On her specific instructions we all received Valium each night for one month after going-through. One of the foster girls, Mechalia, was also given lithium because of her uneasy mental state. Mechalia was the adopted daughter of one of the cult members and was reputed to have behavioural problems.

For a period of about six years our daily vitamin dose was staggering. Each day we had to take twenty-eight yeast tablets, twelve kelp, two vitamin C, two white and one oily vitamin E, one desiccated liver and half a B-forte tablet. We took this sized dose two and three times a day.

The end of the massive vitamin doses coincided with the death of a prominent cult member, Marion Vilimek, whom we knew as Joan Vilimek and who owned the Newhaven Private Psychiatric Hospital in Kew. We believed that Joan Vilimek was supplying the money to buy our vitamins; it was certainly inconceivable that Anne would dig in her own pocket to provide anything other than the occasional bizarre gifts and dresses she bought for us.

Being ill brought few pay-offs for us children. It did not result in appropriate medication or extra emotional support and affection. In fact, it often led to punishment rather than sympathy. For instance, David, who had chronic asthma and a history of allergies, was punished by the Aunties for coughing and wheezing all the time. He was never given bronchodilators, such as Ventolin, or steroids – the proper treatment for his condition. He was just told that he was a wheezer, as if this was something that was his fault. If he woke the Aunties at night with his coughing or wheezing, they would often tip water over him and lock him outside the house for the rest of the night, or just belt him. Often he slept in the bathroom because of his 'noise'. He was even denied meals as a deterrent. Symptoms of any illness were dismissed by Anne and the Aunties as 'all in the mind' or 'attention-seeking' and if someone was really sick he or she tended to be ignored completely.

Homoeopathic remedies, prescribed by Anne, were given to us regularly for all sorts of reasons. Anne proclaimed herself an expert on this form of treatment and told us she had studied it for six years in Tibet. For the affliction of 'disobedience' we were given stramonium; for 'shock' (a term meaning either physical or emotional upset) the treatment was aconite; for 'thinking wrongly', pulsatilla; for 'rocking at night' and for farting, nux vomica. These homoeopathic medicines were administered in addition to our usual punishments for offences, and in addition to other drugs.

I never had a medical consultation with a doctor while taking prescription drugs and, as far as I know, no doctor prescribed these medications for me.

Spinal manipulation was another of Anne's health fads. About 1985 or 1986, when I was 15 or 16, we were taken to see a Doctor Gorman, who specialised in spinal manipulation. Anne told us Doctor Gorman was a genius who could make us better behaved. He could even cure blindness and epilepsy, she said. She had referred quite a few cult members to him, and she decided that we would also benefit from treatment. I don't remember where he practised from, but I think it was somewhere in Ringwood. We were taken to Crowther House, one of Anne's houses in the Dandenongs, from where we were driven across to Doctor Gorman's surgery.

During our initial consultations Anne was always present and a lot of medically irrelevant questions were asked such as 'Do you feel like running away?' and 'How often do you feel like being disobedient?'. A lot of the questions required just yes or no answers, and Anne would often answer them for us. I found the questions quite strange at the time and now, having studied medicine I find them even stranger.

Doctor Gorman said his treatment would help us, but he made no mention of spinal manipulation. He said his treatment would improve my poor eyesight and also my disobedience and impertinence. (I also suffered from a stiff neck and occasional headaches but I think these were probably because I wasn't given glasses for myopia until I was fourteen. The Aunties finally realised I might be short-sighted when, during an astronomy lesson, I couldn't see the stars.)

A couple of weeks after the first interview session, a group of us were told we had to go back to see Doctor Gorman. Before the visit we were not allowed to eat for a day and we were given Valium and Mogadon. Again we stayed at Crowther and were driven to Doctor Gorman's by the Aunties in a couple of cars.

I think I was one of the first to see Doctor Gorman. In the room with him were an anaesthetist, a nurse and a couple of Family members. I remember feeling nervous and uneasy that day, and it could have been because Jim Macfarlane, a physiotherapist and prominent cult member who occasionally visited Uptop, was there. For some reason he always made me feel uncomfortable. When he visited Winberra when I was little I used to hide in a cupboard to avoid seeing him. I think I know why, but I find it too hard to talk about and am unsure about my hazy memories.

I was made to lie down on an operating table in the middle of the room. The anaesthetist put a strap around my arm but had trouble finding a vein and made some remark about plump teenagers and they all laughed. Eventually he found one and stuck the needle in, started counting to ten, and I don't remember anything else until I woke up. I was then in quite a lot of pain, which seemed to extend through my whole body. I had a terrible headache, felt nauseated, and had to be helped to the waiting room of the clinic. I remember hearing Cassandra crying and screaming when she woke up and yelling, 'It hurts, it hurts', over and over. Arrianne and Anna were also crying after their treatments.

When we got back to Crowther House all of us were in a lot of pain. Some children could barely move and lay in bed for days. They hardly ate during this time. I was in a fair bit of pain, particularly in my neck and shoulders, but I got up and walked around: as usual I was trying to present a tough image. I found that the treatment did nothing to improve my eyesight (or my disobedience) and I was left with the painful neck and shoulders. The headaches went on as before.

Anna had furtively looked in during one of the treatments and had seen Cassandra put into a terrible position. Anna said she was lying on her stomach and her legs were being pulled up backwards by Doctor Gorman until they were touching her head. Apparently our bodies had been contorted into weird positions that would not have been possible without a general anaesthetic. Anne said she was going to have spinal manipulation herself, but I don't know if she ever did. I know it was expensive and lots of people in the cult did have it on her orders. Anne was always telling others to do things that she never did herself.

Later there was gossip among cult members that a child had died under spinal manipulation by Doctor Gorman and that he had run away to Western Australia. I am not sure if this was true.

Cassandra was our youngest sister and about seven or eight years younger than me. In some ways I saw her as a symbol of all the children Uptop; she was the most powerless member of our group and the methods used to control her were starvation and drugs. She had lived at Winberra with Aunty Ilene initially and was sometimes brought Uptop to visit us. I remember her as a big, bouncing, bright baby. She was certainly a very young baby when Anne went over to England for about eighteen months. On Anne's return, Cassandra had just started to say some words, but she stopped suddenly. She was to remain mute for a number of years.

We found out the reason for this much later. I remember Anne was combing my hair by the fireplace in the lounge-room just before brunch on a winter's day, when she told us this story. She had returned from England after her long absence and was staying at Winberra. One day, Cassandra was in her high-chair and Aunty Ilene was feeding her. Anne tried to put some food in Cassandra's mouth but Cassandra grabbed the spoon and started waving it around, sending food flying everywhere. Anne was furious. To punish Cassandra for this show of 'disobedience', Anne had taken her out of her high-chair and given her the biggest belting she had ever given anyone. She told us that she had 'really laid into her', and she had had to be stopped by one of the Aunties for fear that Cassandra would be killed. It was from this moment that Cassandra stopped talking and became withdrawn. The Aunties were standing around listening to Anne telling this story and they all voiced their approval. I remember their chorus 'Good on you Anne, they need to be taught from an early age', and how unilaterally supportive they were of Anne as she described, almost boastfully, how she'd 'laid into' a 2-year-old child.

This episode remains clearly in my mind, because although, at the time, I was totally indoctrinated by Anne, I still thought this was a vile thing for anyone to be saying, to brag about. I could not agree with the Aunties that what Anne had done was right, just because of her exalted status as Master. Looking back, I am surprised she told us about it because she herself admitted that she might have overdone the punishment. Anne never usually admitted to mistakes, so this was a very rare occurrence. In hindsight, I actually think she told us to reinforce to everyone around her that day that her power was absolute and that her infamous temper was to be greatly respected and feared.

Cassandra's speech came back all of a sudden in the early 1980s. I remember we were in the United States, all piled in Anne's car on the way to the ashram for the evening darshan with Baba. Anne asked a question and someone answered, in a complete and clear sentence. We all looked around to see who had spoken, not recognising the voice. To our amazement it was Cassandra. Previously she had only said a word or two and had just cried instead of talking. From then on, she spoke normally.

A couple of years after Cassandra did begin talking, she started having fits. During these attacks she would lose consciousness and neither touch nor infliction of pain would elicit a response. In an effort to assess the level of her unconsciousness on these occasions, the Aunties sometimes used to prick Cassandra with a pin, but she would not respond.

Because Cassandra had a round face, Anne decided she was fat and imposed a strict diet. Cassandra ate even less than we did. She got one piece of fruit for breakfast, half a cup of vegetables for lunch, and then a very small salad, consisting of something like half a tomato, a lettuce leaf, a small piece of celery and a small piece of carrot, at night. Even if we were given something different for dinner, Cassandra always got salad. After dinner we might receive two biscuits, but Cassandra did not. Hers was a diet extremely low in even basic nutrients.

At one point Anne decided that Cassandra was too fat because her belly stuck out. A more stringent diet was imposed with the aim of reducing her weight to below 20 kilograms. I remember how Aunty Wynn and Aunty Liz gloated in the mornings when they weighed Cassandra's little stick-like body and then cut her food portions back even further. We needed special dispensation from Anne to give any food to Cassandra. I remember begging Anne to let her have some soup when we had some. But no, Anne had decided her weight had to stay under 20 kilograms until she was a certain height, which I think was about 120 centimetres. I know it seems incredible, but Peter Pan, one of our cats, weighed more than Cassandra. I know this because we had to weigh the cats for worming and Peter Pan, a very large cat, was more than 20 kilograms.

Cassandra was always pale and lethargic. She crept around the house and rarely had any energy to do anything. Sometimes she just lay down and couldn't get up, even when the Aunties screamed at her and beat her, accusing her of putting on an act to get sympathy. They said her comas were due to diabetes and the diet would cure them. They said Anne had placed her on a special diet because she was ill and if we broke the diet we'd be 'following her coffin to the grave'. We believed them. Sometimes, however, we took the risk because, looking at her, it seemed that she would probably die anyway. I think if Cassandra had not scavenged in the rubbish bins and eaten the bread and seed left out for the birds she surely would have died, because that diet was not enough to sustain anyone for long.

For a period between 1985 and 1986 Cassandra was made to sleep upstairs in Anne's bedroom by herself so that she couldn't get out at night to try to steal food. Aunty Helen slept outside the door. When Cassandra wanted to go to the toilet she had to knock on the door to wake Helen in order to be let out. When Anne was overseas I would beg and plead with her on the phone to let Cassandra have a little bit more food. I would tell her that Cassandra was starving. Anne would say that this was nonsense, that we only had to look at Cassandra's big, fat stomach to realise she was well fed indeed. Cassandra's big stomach was due to malnutrition, not to being overweight. I told Anne about kwashiorkor syndrome, which afflicts children in the Third World due to malnutrition, causing their stomachs to bloat. I looked the facts up in biology books and would read relevant passages to Anne. I told her that the swelling was due to oedema due to protein deficiency. Anne completely refused to listen to me. 'Oh, no', she said. 'She's just fat. She has always been fat.' There was nothing that would change her mind.

The Aunties knew there was something seriously wrong with Cassandra because they kept a special observation book for recording her pulse, blood pressure, reflexes and response to pain. We were constantly blamed for Cassandra's fits, just as we were blamed for Stephen's epilepsy – it was God punishing us for our bad behaviour. Now I think Cassandra's comas were due to her extremely poor diet (I am sure she suffered severe hypoglycaemia as a result) and the extreme emotional deprivation to which she was subjected.

Anne said that Cassandra's fits were caused by us locking her in a cupboard once when she was young. Yet it had been Anne who ordered us to put Cassandra in a cupboard if she cried continually. I remember, with Andrea and Susanne, following these instructions, not in a spirit of cruelty, but more as troops just following orders. Maybe we were not so far from becoming honorary Aunties ourselves at times. Later Anne began exaggerating the story, saying we had hung Cassandra in the cupboard, which was not true. I now feel bad about shutting her in the cupboard but at the time I didn't give it a second thought. But Anne was a clever manipulator; she got to me then and I believed for a long time that it was my fault that Cassandra had fits. It was just another example of how we were made to take the blame for anything bad that happened.

In an attempt to cure Cassandra of her attacks, Anne and the Aunties began using imported drugs on her. The drugs came from Germany and were meant to make her grow. At the time I thought they were steroids because two of the other kids, Timothy and Arrianne, had been given a course of steroids to encourage their growth. I know this because Doctor Christabel Wallace and the other Aunties called these drugs steroids. Anne had wanted Arrianne, in particular, to grow because she was very small, but she never grew much. I think her growth was actually halted by the early doses of steroids given to her.

Cassandra was given her drugs with big syringes. This was quite a process, often taking between five and ten minutes. The injections went into her bottom and they were very painful because she had almost no flesh on her. We were called on to hold her down while she was injected and she used to scream. I remember her poor skinny little behind being covered with bruises. But the Aunties said the injections were to help Cassandra get better and we believed them. We later found out, after we had left Uptop, that these injections were of homoeopathic mixtures of animal organs. Cassandra was given two of these mixtures, one called Neycalm, the other Neychondrim. One of them was designed to treat joint pain, the other to counteract hypersexuality in children. The concoctions included extracts from animal thymus gland, hypophyseal gland, spinal medulla, adrenal gland, testis, liver, pancreas, fat and kidney. I'm not sure how Anne thought they would help Cassandra to grow: perhaps she thought, in her disordered way, that all

Cassandra's problems were of a sexual nature. Needless to say, these horrible injections had no effect on Cassandra's growth.

I regularly had nightmares about Cassandra's tiny wasted body, so when I got a chance to help her, I did. Cassandra is one of the main reasons I eventually talked to the police when I left Uptop.

CHAPTER 6

All creatures great and small

Anne believed animals were spirits evolving into humans or even spirits higher in the karmic evolutionary scale than humans, sent to watch over us. While children were dominated and treated with disdain and revulsion, animals were special and were treated with reverence.

There were always cats around and, to a degree, they were a comfort to us and we loved them – at least we had something to cuddle. They were very important to us because they were our only source of affection. Each one of us would try to coax them into bed at night so we could snuggle up to them. To this day I find it easier to be affectionate to cats than to humans.

At Uptop there were nine cats, at Winberra twenty-five. The males were never neutered, but the females were all spayed, which again tells you something about Anne's priorities. The males used to fight a lot and spray urine all around the house.

At Broom Farm, Anne's Tudor mansion in England, there was a cattery, which housed about twenty-five cats. On reflection, it can't have been much of a life for them: they didn't get let out often. However, they were part of Anne's scheme. They were important – souls in transition – and it was our job to look after them. In addition, there were about ten house cats at Broom Farm. They had the complete run of things and could go anywhere around the mansion. We, on the other hand, were restricted to the less posh areas of the house. When I was over in England, it was my job to feed all these cats in the early morning, and it was quite a time-consuming task.

The animals always had the best food. They ate better than the Aunties and certainly better than us children. The cats had cooked chicken and fish and the dogs ate cooked T-bone steak. If there were no adults around, Cassandra, David and Julieanne frequently ate the food put out for the animals. I think all of us did on occasions.

There were two dogs that I particularly remember at Eildon – Joshua, a black Labrador, and Girly, a blue heeler. The Aunties had found Girly one day swimming in the lake, looking for her drowned pups it was said, and we took her in. I think she then directed all her maternal feelings to us kids because, whenever we were getting a belting, the Aunties had to muzzle her to stop her attacking them. She loved us and protected us fiercely.

Joshua was another story. He was on the Aunties' side. He would get into a frenzy during a belting and try to bite us. I can remember being more terrified of his bites than the actual belting at times. Joshua and Girly had massive dog fights, and it was a constant battle to keep them separated during troubled times.

We remembered the date and time, even to the second, of the deaths of our animals. With a morbid solemnity, we observed the anniversaries of their deaths. I remember the day Joshua died. He was comatose upstairs for a lot of the day and we were only allowed up two at a time to sit beside his bedside. Although he had sided against us in disputes with the Aunties, we were still fond of him. I remember being on my knees in the downstairs girls' bedroom and praying desperately to God to save him. I tried to bargain with God to intervene but, as usual, He never listened to my pleas.

When Joshua died, we were told it was our fault – it was because we were so sinful. He was taken into Anne's room and for three days we had to sit around him in a vigil, praying beside this dead dog, with incense burning and Handel's 'Largo' playing in the background. It was the middle of summer and after a few days Joshua started to stink. At dawn on the fourth day we buried him in the garden, a ritual that was supposed to allow his soul to move onto its next level more easily. This ritual was observed with all the animals that died Uptop.

Doggy-boy came to us in about 1976 or 1977 when Bill brought him back from Alexandra, a town about 30 kilometres from Eildon. He said he'd found the dog wandering around, apparently lost. Some years later, maybe in 1980 or 1981, Doggy-boy was involved inadvertently in an incident that further demonstrated the priority given to animals over us. Bill was Uptop for Christmas, although Anne was overseas. Bill's presence caused a lot of excitement because we only ever got presents at Christmas on the very rare occasions when either he or Anne was at home.

Bill's mother visited him at Uptop just prior to Christmas and gave him a basket of fudge for us. He told us about the fudge and we were delighted. He said we could have a piece the next day, which was Christmas Day. He left the fudge on the kitchen bench and before he went to bed he noticed a piece or two had been stolen. He was furious and stormed down to us in bed to say that if the culprits did not own up by the morning we would all get 'six of the best'. We knew this meant a massive belting with a heavy leather belt, a common enough punishment meted out by both Bill and Leon. It meant leaning over the black stool, or their knees when we were younger, and getting the hardest whacks they could give. Of course it never ended up just being 'six of the best' as they would work themselves into a frenzy and lay into us until they were exhausted.

Understandably we were very scared by Bill's threat and although we were meant to be asleep we had a meeting in the downstairs corridor to try to get the fudge thief to own up. We decided that it was Julieanne and Timothy who had taken it and we tried to get them to confess. Julieanne owned up readily but said she'd given her piece to Doggy-boy. As the Aunties discovered that Doggy-boy had vomited and that the vomit contained fudge, Julieanne was given special dispensation. This meant that Timothy had to take the full blame.

I remember the belting Timothy got the next morning before brunch. Bill took off his belt and put Timothy over his knee. Bill went berserk. He was calling Timothy 'a little bastard', and yelling and screaming in a mostly incoherent rage. I remember counting the strokes and there were well over twenty. After the belting Timothy was sent to bed for the rest of the weekend and we weren't allowed to speak to him at all. We never did have the fudge for Christmas.

When Doggy-boy came, we already had Joshua and Girly, so his addition meant further friction between the dogs. One evening the dogs had been fighting and it was particularly difficult to keep them apart so Bill locked Doggy-boy in the Valiant for the night with the windows up. The next morning when we went out to see him, he'd had a stroke and appeared to be paralysed and close to death. We took him inside and laid him on a mattress in the lounge-room and that was his kingdom for the next ten years until his death.

It was part of the Aunties' job to take Doggy-boy out to relieve himself in the morning and at night and it was part of our job to go and talk to Doggy-boy during the day. The other dogs were not allowed into the lounge-room after the incident. Over time Doggy-boy achieved a little more movement and in the end he could drag himself around a bit. He was a very gutsy dog. After a few years he appeared to be getting steadily better until Anne got the Aunties to take him to Melbourne for some spinal manipulation. When he came back he was worse than he had ever been and never attempted to walk again. When he died, a couple of years after Joshua, we were blamed for his death. He, too, was laid out on Anne's bed for three days after he died.

Dinky-dog was an animal with an unstable and sometimes ferocious personality. He would go for our feet under the table and I was always worried that he would bite me. He had a dreadful habit of sniffing around the sewerage. One day Ben called Dinky a 'sewer dog' and Anne decided that this meant Ben had a mind like a sewer and therefore should be dipped in raw sewage. After a belting, Bill took Ben out to dunk him in the septic tank, which was situated away from the house and covered by a concrete slab. Ben was screaming as he was taken away and Julieanne was crying – she was particularly upset because Ben was supposed to be her twin.

We all believed Ben was going to be dunked in the sewage. What apparently transpired was that Bill removed the slab and held Ben by his ankles over the raw sewage and then, at the last moment, gave him a reprieve. Poor Ben, I remember him, pale and shaking, telling me and some of the other children about it later. It was another lesson for us about our place in the scheme of things. We lived in a world where even to insult a dog was liable to get you into enormous trouble.

We had a lot of different dogs and cats over the years and I bear the animals no grudges: I still have fond memories of them. It wasn't their fault that Anne had some strange notions about them.

When I was 6 or 7, there was an horrific incident involving bull ants at Uptop. Some of the children had been playing outside and were caught poking sticks into ant holes. I wasn't there at the time and the first I heard of it was when we were all told to gather in the lounge-room. There would have been ten or more children, all of us sitting on the couch, and a lot of visitors. The visitors must have been special cult members invited for the day otherwise they wouldn't have been allowed to see us. They may not have been strictly core members because it was early days. Later, Uptop became quite secret and only a chosen few were allowed to visit.

The ants incident was taken very seriously by Anne because two rules had been broken: first, we were not allowed to pick up sticks or stones; and second, we were forbidden to be cruel to animals. Anne, sensing the moment, went into full preaching mode. She visibly gathered herself together and imperiously lectured us on cruelty to animals. Remember, all the adults revered her and completely supported her point of view. She went on and on about the breaking of these two important rules and finally announced that because we had hurt the animals, she was going to hurt us.

She had decided, she said, to put bull ants down our backs. The thought of this was terrifying to everyone. I'd been bitten by bull ants many times in the past and still remembered the pain of the bites. They were very common in our playground – they marched down from several nests on the hill. Anne knew how frightened we were but she kept going, hoping to instil as much fear in us as possible. She described in loving detail the pain of bull ant bites, how the lumps would come up all hard and red, and how they would be agony for days afterwards. Anne could be very theatrical at times and all around her were transfixed by her performance that day.

She sent two of the men out into the garden to fill up a jar with bull ants. While they were outside she continued to enlarge on her theme – how the ants themselves would enjoy our tender skin, how we deserved ongoing pain because of our thoughtless, cruel actions against these defenceless creatures who had caused us no harm. I remember sitting there, squashed up against the others, waiting for the ants to be delivered and poured down my back. I was filled with fear.

The two men returned with a jam jar containing about ten to twenty swarming, angry-looking bull ants. They gave the jar to Anne and she held it up for us all to see. With great drama she asked for a volunteer from among the children: who would be the first to have bull ants poured down his or her back?

We were silent. I doubt whether I would have been able to speak let alone step forward. Then John stood up, shaking all over yet saying that, because he was the eldest, he would volunteer to be first. I remember being staggered by his bravery. I know I could not have done it that day.

John walked over to Anne. He was white as a sheet, trembling, barely able to totter. Anne, maliciously enjoying the whole scene, theatrically opened the lid of the jam jar. Her movements were slow and exaggerated. I believed completely that she was going to tip the bull ants down John's back and I felt sick with terror. Some of the younger children began to cry and I felt like crying myself.

After drawing out this build-up as long as she could, Anne decided against tipping the bull ants down John's back and put the lid back on. She said something about not going ahead with the threats because of John's bravery. But now, she said, we knew what would happen if we ever did such a thing to the poor defenceless bull ants again. The grown-ups in the room were all laughing at what they considered to be Anne's wit and our manifest terror. How magnetic she was, holding us all in her power.

I still have nightmares about bull ants crawling over my skin. Is that because I was an over-sensitive child? Do the others have similar dreams? The nightmares do not come as often now, but I continue to have a phobia about ants. If one gets on my skin, I flick it off but still feel a prickly sensation for a few hours afterwards, and I slap myself to get the imaginary insects off me. Being forced to take a lot of hallucinogenic drugs as a child does not help in resolving delusions such as these.

CHAPTER 7

Outsiders

People within the cult were always paranoid about outsiders and The Family's motto 'Unseen, Unheard, Unknown' reflected their paranoia. In the late 1970s, the cult became the object of some media attention. Because of complaints by people who had 'lost' family members to Anne, public awareness of the cult's activities gradually increased. In 1980 media attention focused on the Kim Halm case. Kim Halm was the daughter of Family members. When her father left the cult he lost trace of her and tried for three years to track her down. The Federal police were involved in the search for Kim and eventually they came sniffing around Uptop. This made life even more miserable for us.

To make matters worse, another former cult member named George had gone to the newspapers. He had been one of our 'Uncles' in the early days at Uptop, when life had been easier and the discipline less harsh. I remember, however, that none of us liked him very much. He used to be fond of lining the girls up against Anne's big red bed in the lounge-room, pulling down their underwear and slapping their bare backsides with his hands. He was thought to be Arrianne's natural father and he started making attempts to get her back. As a result, we weren't allowed outside at all for a few months.

Things were very tense. Imagine up to thirty children living in a small house and none of them ever being able even to go outside to play. I remember pressing my nose against the fly-screen of the downstairs outside door after one of the Aunties told me to 'get some fresh air'. Our only exercise during that period consisted of daily Hatha yoga, some exercises in the girls' room at lunchtime, and pacing up and down the small downstairs hallway – an activity in which we all indulged. These days I still pace around when I am feeling stressed.

Because Uptop was not registered as a school until 1984, cult members had to keep our existence a secret. The Aunties convinced us that there would be terrible repercussions if the police found us, so we had to be very quiet during the week and stay inside a lot. The Aunties persuaded us that we would be the ones who got into trouble if the police did come. I thought that if the police caught us they would put us in a big bag and beat us. I believed that we would be taken away and repeatedly beaten in dark prison cells. We were frightened of all strangers, but we were terrified of police. So when anyone came to Uptop we were silent.

Although it was Anne who originally ordered that we be hidden from view, I think it was Liz Whitaker who first dreamed up the idea of stuffing us into a small enclosed area under the house. Access was through one of the downstairs bedrooms. One corner of the boys' bedroom led into a small room that housed a pump used for pumping water to the house from the lake. In the wall of the pump-room was a hole about 60 centimetres square. This led into a small area under the house, with a dirt floor and earthen sides. It was really just a cavity under the house formed by the way the house had been built into the hill. The hole in the pump-room wall was covered with a picture: a little wooden-framed picture with boats on it. When visitors, tradespeople or police came, we had to climb into the underground area, then the picture was placed over the hole again.

The hiding area was very small, about a metre high and 2 metres wide. It was not visible from the door that opened into the area under the house at the opposite end. The police, or anyone else looking in from that vantage point, would have only seen a stretcher and some rubbish piled up. They would not have seen the place beyond the stretcher where we hid. And no one would have ever thought to look behind the picture in the pump-room if they were searching the house.

The small area was rocky and dusty, full of cob-webs and spiders. When the alarm was given, we all had to clamber in there as fast as possible. It was a dark and suffocating place, especially if you were unlucky enough to be at the bottom of the pile. Once in, we were not allowed to make any noise. If we did, we would be in serious trouble. But we did not need threats to keep us quiet: our fear of the police was more than enough.

At Anne's direction, the Aunties held drill practices, so that at the sound of a warning whistle or bell we moved quickly into our positions. If the police arrived during the day while we were in the schoolroom, we had to dismantle the trestle tables and put the books in boxes and cover them with blankets. We had to make the room look like the uninhabited bedroom of a holiday house, then climb through the hole in the pump-room wall, one on top of the other. We got the drill down to a fine art and were able to pack up the schoolroom and get into our hiding place within two or three minutes.

If we were in bed when the police arrived, we were woken, made to straighten our bed covers, push in the trundle beds, and fold up the stretcher beds and put them in cupboards. An Aunty usually helped the boys, who were slow at waking. Then we had to change into tracksuits if there was time. If there was none, we went straight to the pump-room in our pyjamas and climbed into the dark hole, making not a single noise. We had to do this while the Aunties were entertaining the police, often with cups of tea. Once the police left, we were allowed out. There were quite a few visits by the police, so we had lots of practices. When the police visits died down so did the drill sessions.

We met the police on one of their visits. I don't know why we had not been forced to hide, but I suppose that it must have been the school holidays or a weekend. At that stage we were supposed to be attending schools in Melbourne and we had been briefed about what we should say if anyone asked us questions.

I remember two policemen, one of them in uniform. We were called upstairs for the interview, and we all sat in the lounge-room opposite and as far away as possible from the cops sitting in the armchairs. I remember Stephen burying his head in a cushion because he was so terrified. He relaxed a bit when one policeman showed him his digital watch. Stephen, who had always loved gadgets, was very interested. Aunty Wynn and Liz Whitaker were there I think.

The police asked us if we were happy with our treatment and whether we were well fed. We answered 'Yes' to all their questions. We were asked our names, ages and what schools we attended. The girls all chorused Camberwell Girls' Grammar School and the boys said Kingswood College. Stephen was the only exception; he said he went to Xavier. We all looked up because we knew Stephen was not supposed to say that, but the Aunties covered up for him, saying that because he was a bit 'different' he went to a different school.

We would never have imagined saying anything other than what the Aunties drilled us to say. We were to lie to outsiders, telling them that we only came to Uptop on the weekends. We complied totally. For a start we thought the world was a terrible place – our own experience was proof – and secondly we'd been told the police were the worst people in the world and would take us away and torture us. We didn't want anything to do with them and we certainly wouldn't have volunteered any information. All we wanted was for them to go away and leave us to the tender mercies of Uptop and the Aunties. I can only assume the police didn't check out the details we gave them because nothing happened.

I can never really forgive those two young cops who interviewed us that day. If they had been a little more observant, if they had listened a little harder or probed a little more, maybe we would have been saved from many more years Uptop. Not only that: if the police force had checked out our stories, they would have discovered that we did not attend any schools in Melbourne.

In 1978, when I was about 8, we were all baptised at St Mary's Catholic Church in Alexandra. We were questioned on our knowledge of the Bible by the priest, whose name was Father Griffin. We knew our Bible fairly well because we read it a lot. The next Sunday we got all dressed up and went to the church where we were baptised with holy water. I remember the holy water being being sprinkled over us by the priest and then names were read out, names that were supposed to be ours. Some of them were long like Cassandra Clare Francesca. We all had a first name, followed by two middle names, and then Hamilton-Byrne.

I think Anne had us baptised so she could use our baptismal certificates for passport purposes. I don't think she insisted on the ceremony for religious reasons for we were hardly Christians. We went to church at Easter if Bill was there, but never at Christmas.

In 1980, when I was about 10 or 11, we went to the Dandenong Festival, and this developed into an annual outing. For the first few years we played piano pieces. Initially only the boys went because they were the best piano players. They had started lessons at a younger age than the girls because Anne considered them, by dint of being male, superior to us girls. Then we were all allowed to join in, and we were entered in various sections of the competition. We started singing at the festival in 1983, and singing became a big part of our lives. We practised every day before lunch. Close to festival time, singing took on a more prominent part in our daily routine, and we practised it instead of doing schoolwork. For a week before a singing performance we ate only fruit and drank only water, as Anne believed that would make our voices more pure.

I didn't like singing lessons much. I also didn't like the speech lessons to make us sound like an English person. When I was older – I think I was about 14 – I became quite subversive in some ways and, along with some of the others, fought to be allowed to call Anne 'Mum' instead of the English 'Mummy'. In the end we got permission for this.

We would travel down to Crowther House the day before the Dandenong Festival. We loved going to Crowther, partly because it provided such a welcome interruption to the monotony of our daily routine. The house was a rambling mansion, in those days run by cult members as a tea house. People would go there to have Devonshire teas and cult members would wait on them. It was probably quite a money-spinner for Anne.

If we did well at the Dandenong Festival, after the performance Anne would let us return to Crowther and stay a couple more days. If she was particularly happy with our competition results we had a party at Crowther when we got back, with cakes, biscuits and sandwiches – delicious food, or 'Aunty food' as we termed it, that was otherwise unheard of in our lives.

At the Dandenong Festival, and during any other times we interacted with the outside world, we were forbidden to talk to anyone unless directly approached. We had been well drilled in what our responses to questions were to be in such instances. If anyone asked where we were from we had to say that we attended a boarding school called Aquinel College. Sometimes other children who were competing would come up and try to talk with us. They might say 'Hi', or comment that Cassandra, 'the little one', was cute. We'd just reply that she was our sister; we were forbidden to volunteer any other information. At times the other competitors giggled at us and mocked us for our daggy, old-fashioned, frilly blue and white uniforms, made by Aunty Wynn to be worn only on these occasions. They ridiculed our stilted, awkward manners, our silly English voices and our white hair, which made us look like something out of *The Sound of Music*. They called us 'albinos', which hurt deeply because we did not want to appear strange.

I wished that I could speak to those other children. I was vaguely attracted to them, although they seemed pretty rough and noisy and Anne compared them unfavourably with us, saying they were uncouth and common and undisciplined. Seeing them made us feel quite isolated and different.

We did quite well at the Dandenong Festival. Luke and Cassandra won prizes for their piano playing, and we got an honourable mention for our singing two years in a row. Overall we rather enjoyed doing well and making Anne and Bill proud of us. That was worth the boredom of all the practice sessions and going on a fruit diet.

While I lived at Uptop, I travelled to England three times and to the United States a few times, to Hawaii and to Fallsburg in the Catskill Mountains of New York State. Anne owned property in both England and the States. In England we stayed at Broom Farm in Kent. I still cannot work out why Anne took us on these trips. It was certainly more exciting than the routine at Uptop. But, when I think back on Anne's behaviour and general attitude towards us, it seems unlikely that she would spend money on taking us overseas just so that we could have fun or spend time with someone for whom we had great affection.

Whatever Anne's reasons for taking us overseas, life there was much better than at Uptop, although we still lived a fairly isolated existence. In the Catskills Baba Muktananda's ashram was just down the road and we had trips there every day, while in the evenings we were able to join in activities with the other disciples at the ashram. As I have said, Baba also granted us a private audience or darshan, once a week, coming over to Anne's house to see us, and was very good to us. We worshipped and adored him – we wanted nothing better than to stay at his feet forever. In retrospect, it was remarkable that he gave us so much time and attention because at that time he was very famous and had many thousands of devotees worldwide, and lots of demands for his time and attention.

Once Baba asked us if we wanted to leave Anne and go and

stay with him in his ashram in Ganeshpuri. We all enthusiastically said yes, and were later belted and abused by Anne for being so disloyal. I am not sure if he ever knew or guessed what our life was like: he certainly never criticised Anne and treated her with a lot of respect apart from occasionally playing practical jokes on her. Once he gave Anne a sari, frightfully garish and not at all to her taste. He insisted she try it on and parade in front of everyone. She tried to decline, but Baba would not take no for an answer, so she reluctantly complied. We were highly amused by this, as was Baba, knowing what a blow the parade was to Anne's vanity. We had great difficulty stifling our laughter.

I don't understand why or how Anne got involved with Baba. He certainly paid her a lot of attention. In the end she caused a lot of trouble in the ashram, and several of Baba's close disciples defected to The Family, including two prominent swamis. Maybe Anne approached his sect because she saw an opportunity to establish another sphere of influence. I was present when Swami Tajomayananda was initiated by Anne into The Family and, knowing what a wonderful person he was (he had come to stay at Eildon with us for a while), I am still puzzled about why he would want to join a cult where everyone was so miserable, when it seemed to me that everyone around Baba was so happy.

In the United States and England we also had nicer food than at Uptop and occasionally went for drives in the countryside or walks off the property. Not only that, it was good not to have to feel that we were in hiding from the outside world. I remember once playing on the lawns at Broom Farm when a plane flew overhead and being surprised that we didn't have to run inside, as we would have done Uptop.

Despite this generally better lifestyle, the stays in the Catskills were a time of emotional ups and downs for me. Although Anne let us have more fun and privileges and spent a lot more time with us, she could still be very cruel: not physically so much as mentally. For example, she knew that we loved Baba deeply and so held over us the power that she could stop us seeing him at any time she wished.

Once Andrea and I wrote a poem to Baba, expressing our devotion to him as disciples, and gave it to him at our private darshan. He had it read to him by his interpreter and then insisted we read it out at the large public darshan that night. Anne was forced to praise us in front of him and allow us to read it in public. It was only later that evening, after we got home, that she expressed her anger that we had written a poem without consulting her. For this crime she ordered that we be punished and we received a belting from Bill in front of a lot of the cult members. Before we had our belting they stood around and mocked Baba in front of us. I remember feeling more angry at their rudeness to Baba, my guru, than at the injustice of the belting. I knew the Guru Gita by heart then, and I remember finding consolation in the verse that said that those who slander the Guru's name will burn in hell 'so long as the sun and the moon remain' and be born in Hell in a demon's form, to thirst for water unceasingly. I could not understand how the adults could be so hypocritical; could receive Baba's darshan and then make fun of him behind his back. To me there could be no such position in between: the grace and love of Baba permeated my whole life. I could not worship him one moment and forget him the next.

During this visit to the Catskill Mountains, Anne initiated a system aimed at recording our crimes by means of a chart kept on the lounge-room wall. All our names were listed, and the Aunties who were there had to enter all the alleged misdemeanours that we got up to during that day. Anne would review this with the Aunties every night (which was generally the only time of the day that we would see her) and then hand out the punishments: usually missing seeing Baba that night, or a belting, or lines.

When we returned to Eildon after this trip Andrea and I, in particular, were filled with devotion to Baba. He offered us spiritual solace; a refuge from the harsh reality of the world in which we lived. By meditation, chanting and repeating the mantra we could transcend what was going on around us, and find happiness in worshipping God and a guru. We built a mini 'ashram' in the yard and set up altars to Baba everywhere. We wanted badly to do guruseva for Baba and so built this 'ashram' (in reality only a cleared corner of our yard) with great reverence for him, clearing away every leaf and stone and surrounding the boundaries with small, white pebbles. We called ourselves by the spiritual names that he had given us. We meditated intensely on him and chanted at every opportunity we got. Soon, however, our 'ashram' was dismantled and we were forbidden from engaging in devotions except at the times of day designated for such activities. We had apparently been deriving far too much joy from our faith and devotion to Baba. Perhaps Anne was getting jealous.

After Uptop received its approval rating as a residential school, Aquinel College, in about 1984, we were visited by inspectors from the Education Department once a year. The Aunties and Uncle Leon must have told many lies to retain the school registration. They invented several years of school reports for us – reports on subjects we did not do – and wrote them for the authorities on Aquinel College notepaper especially prepared for the occasion.

We had to tell the inspectors that we studied in the lounge-room because the light was better there than in the room downstairs that we usually worked in, and that we did normal school subjects like science, biology, chemistry and social studies, which in fact we didn't study or certainly not up to secondary school standard. As I pointed out earlier, the only subjects we did were maths, English and French.

The first time the inspector was due, Leon and Helen brought up science and art posters that other children had done, pasted them around the walls and pretended that it was our work. In later years we made posters ourselves especially for the occasion. It was far removed from the education programme we normally followed. A sports and excursion programme that we supposedly adhered to was also invented.

When the inspector came, we dressed up in our blue and white

Aquinel College uniforms and, adept by now at lying to strangers, parroted the fibs we had been taught. We had to memorise dates of birth and details about our early schools. On one visit the inspector commented that we were quiet children: we were told the next time he came to make as much noise as possible while we were in the 'play yard'.

There was always an incredible amount of tension in the house before the inspector came. We were worried that we would say the wrong thing, or forget the version of events that we were supposed to recite if he questioned us. On the day the inspector came, we were given different meals, and Leon came up and pretended that he was always present there as a teacher. When the inspector left there was always a palpable feeling of relief. The Aunties would ring Anne up in England and report on how the visit had gone, how we had successfully fooled the authorities into letting Aquinel College continue for another year.

CHAPTER 8

My mother, my master

Among the many things that Anne told us was that she was a direct descendant of the French royal family. The royal blood was, she said, on her mother's side. She described her mother as a small woman with red hair. I think my red hair was what made me special to Anne. She never spoke much about her mother, except about her hair and the fact that she was Scottish and came from the Hamilton clan. Anne hung the Hamilton coat of arms on the wall at Winberra.

Anne said that her father was an inventor and was good friends with an 'English explorer [sic] – a fellow who went over to Arabia and lived with the natives and his name was Lawrence of Arabia'! As a child, she said, she had lived in a grand mansion with massive grounds. Her father was supposed to have a great castle in Germany and one day we were all going to visit Grandad there.

Anne also said we were indirect descendants of Jesus Christ because, she reasoned, she and therefore her children were from the house of David, which was the house of Jesus. The lineage was all set out in the front of the Bible. She told us that we weren't allowed to tell anyone about this because royalty was no longer popular and we 'might get our heads cut off'! Anne said we should be very proud of our ancestry and it was no wonder we had a guru in the family and that one day one of us would become a guru too. She was constantly telling us that when the right moment came one of us would be chosen, and that she was always watching us to see which one of us was displaying the characteristics of spirituality and potential self-realisation.

There is no evidence to support any of Anne's claims about her heritage. There is no evidence that her stories were anything but fantastic delusions. We knew nothing more about her than these lies, and later the facts about her were hard to come by. I cannot begin to describe how bizarre and surreal it felt when I read in the newspapers about the life of the woman I believed was my own mother and learnt the truth about my own origins. I also cannot adequately describe how bitter and sad I was that she hadn't told us; that I had to learn about my true identity from the media, and not from the woman I had loved as my mother. There was an immense sense of betrayal at how I had been duped for so long.

I discovered later, from researching newspapers, that stories had been written about the cult in the Melbourne *Age* as early as 1983. The cult had first come to the attention of *Age* journalist David Elias purely by accident long before that because he owned land in the Dandenongs opposite the home of Doctor John Mackay, a cult psychiatrist. David Elias first realised there was something strange going on after his daughter had been playing with Helen, Doctor Mackay's daughter. Elias's daughter had told him Helen Mackay 'doesn't just have one mummy, she has lots'.

Gradually Elias became more interested in the cult's activities and in 1979, while he was writing a series on alternative religions, he tried to write something on The Family. He was warned off by Doctor Raynor Johnson, who threatened to sue the paper. Doctor Johnson was at the time a very influential man. He was the retired Master of Melbourne University's Queen's College and was a respected world authority on religion. He was also co-founder with Anne of The Family. After the *Age* was threatened with a writ it took another four years before Elias could come up with anything else on The Family because of the incredible secrecy that surrounded the cult.

The information that he unearthed came from months of digging. He learnt that the woman we knew as Anne Hamilton-Byrne was born Evelyn Grace Victoria Edwards in Sale, Victoria. She was one of seven children born to a railway engine cleaner, Ralph Vernon Edwards, and his English second wife, Florence Louise.

Apparently young Evelyn's mother was known for setting fire to her own curly red hair and for having an interest in psychic phenomena and talking to the dead. Subsequently other journalists have reported that Anne's mother was mentally ill and died alone in a mental asylum. Anne's aunts in England (her mother's sisters) were institutionalised and Anne's sister suffered from psychiatric problems as well.

Newspapers have reported that Anne grew up in a large family. However, after her mother was committed to Ararat Mental Asylum, Anne spent some of her childhood in the Old Brighton Orphanage. Although Anne claims to have gone to Firbank Church of England Grammar School, school records show she began at Grade One at Sunshine Primary School on 7 February 1929 and that she had come there from the orphanage.

Anne has said she was handicapped at school but fellow school pupils do not recall any callipers. In fact, according to newspaper reports, they only remember 'an overweight child whose nickname was "Puddy" '. Perhaps this early childhood teasing goes some way towards explaining Anne's later obsession with dieting and with controlling our food intake and weight.

Anne has claimed to have qualifications in psychiatric nursing, homoeopathy and physiotherapy and to have a pilot's licence. Journalists who have searched the records find no evidence of any of those qualifications. She has also said she was a famous opera singer, winning a Sun Aria award and later studying with Dame Joan Hammond and Dame Joan Sutherland. She also has a number of aliases, including Fiona Macdonald, Anne Hamilton and Michelle Sutherland.

In 1941 Anne married a 24-year-old RAAF policeman named

Don Harris and had her daughter Judith (who later called herself Natasha). Harris was killed in a car accident in 1955. Newspapers report, though with no substantiation, that Harris's death was predicted by a Tibetan guru whom Anne had met earlier. As with anything connected with Anne, it's hard to know the truth.

After her first husband's death, Anne seemed to disappear for four years. Some reports say she spent several years in Geelong, where she gave yoga lessons for a dollar a head in a church hall, then set herself up as a therapist of some sort in Melbourne. It is recorded that in 1959 she enrolled in a yoga class in Melbourne.

At this time she called herself Anne Harris but registered her name as Anne Hamilton. She reportedly was asked to leave the class after putting a 'spell' on a fellow student. In the 1960s she married a former navy officer named Michael Riley and went to live in the Dandenong Ranges just outside Melbourne. Riley worked as Doctor Raynor Johnson's gardener in those days, and this may have been how Anne came to know the man with whom she went on to co-found The Family. Her marriage to Riley did not last long.

Raynor Johnson was a physicist who had spent much of his life studying Eastern mysticism and religion and had written several books on the subject. Apparently Anne appeared at Doctor Johnson's door one Sunday just before the Johnson family were to sit down for their roast dinner. Doctor Johnson took her into his study. After some time he emerged in a state of high excitement. He rushed to his wife and said, 'Mary, she wants to meet you'. This is how The Family was born. We were told Raynor Johnson was our godfather, and I remember a kindly old fellow with white hair who came to visit us sometimes.

In the group that formed around Raynor Johnson and Anne, Doctor Johnson was known as the John the Baptist figure to Anne's Christ. They met on Thursdays and Sundays in the study of his big, old house at Ferny Creek in the hills, and the talk would be of the principles of yoga and meditation. Finally this group became more formal and developed into the beginning of The

Family. They built a place called the Santiniketan Lodge. This had as its namesake the school founded by the Indian mystic and poet Rabindranath Tagore. The lodge was to become Anne's temple in the hills, and the main base of operation for the cult.

The man we took to be our father, Bill Byrne, was an earth-moving contractor from Traralgon in Victoria. In 1968 he took his son Michael to the Newhaven Psychiatric Hospital for treatment. This hospital by then was completely under the influence of Anne, who was a director. As I have said, it was owned by a cult member Joan Vilimek, who acted as matron, and it was staffed in part by psychiatrists, doctors and nurses who were cult members. It didn't take long for Bill to come under Anne's spell and he soon left his wife and moved in with Anne. They married in 1978. Bill had been a local government councillor and was still commuting from Gippsland when the first children were arriving at Winberra.

It has been suggested that Anne would have had no power without a syringe. She claimed a lot of knowledge of medical things. She said she had been the matron of a hospital, but there is no evidence she ever did nursing. I can't emphasise enough the importance that the cult placed on nursing. It was critical in the selection of the Aunties, and it was the profession that Anne planned for the female children. She said nursing was one of the ideal occupations because it was a form of 'selfless service' that led to spiritual advancement. We knew that on their weeks off from Uptop the Aunties were either training to be nurses or practising as nurses. Several of the Aunties nursed Lord Casey, a former governor-general of Australia. Rumour has it that he made a significant donation to the cult.

I have mentioned earlier the alarming drug dependency of the cult and how we were constantly administered prescription drugs. There was always a lot of medical paraphernalia around Uptop: syringes, tablets, and more. I remember one whole cupboard containing hundreds of bottles of homoeopathic medicines. This cupboard was in the downstairs girls' room, and one summer we broke in and stole considerable quantities of these medicines because the pills were sugar coated and tasted like lollies.

I remember thinking when I was a child that we had a beautiful young mother. If ever we asked her how old she was, she would always say she was twenty-one. We tended to believe her because so much about her seemed magical. I didn't question her power over ageing, and because she had facial surgery regularly she never seemed to age. She usually looked about twenty years younger than she was and still does. I guess the fact that we were all supposed to be her biological children, and that Natasha was an adult, should have given us a clue to her age, but as a child you don't look for clues. You just believe what your mother tells you. I know it doesn't make any sense, but we never questioned her.

Anne would go to England and the United States for at least six months of every year and one time stayed away for eighteen months. As I have explained earlier, even when she and Bill were in the country they only visited Uptop intermittently at weekends. However, despite her physical absence from Uptop her presence in our lives was all-pervasive. There were portrait photos of her all around the house, and wherever you were her eyes seemed to follow you. There were little altars to her in the schoolroom and in the lounge-room. We used to spend a large part of our day thinking about her, we prayed to her at night before going to bed, and we believed that she knew our thoughts and was aware of what we were going to do even before we actually did it. And, of course, the books in which she wrote the rules became the bible for our existence.

When Anne was away, we wrote letters telling her our dreams, although there always had to be a first draft of any letter, which was checked over by the Aunties before we rewrote it in our best handwriting. We were never allowed to start a letter with the word 'I' and the first page of the letter had to be on a subject other than ourselves to discourage any display of excessive ego. We waited for a letter or a phone call from her like farmers wait for rain in a drought. If she sent us a letter it was read and reread, dissected for hidden messages and then treasured as an almost sacred communication. Similarly we hung out for her to send us a message that she loved us when she rang on the phone. The whole house would hush in expectation whenever the telephone rang, hoping that it would be her, and that she would say that she was coming to visit us or that she planned to return soon from overseas.

When Anne was in the country she would ring us about once a week. When she was overseas she rang us less frequently, although she spoke to the Aunties much more often. It was a treat for us to be allowed a word with her on these occasions. There was quite a protocol about phone calls. We would be lined up in order of age to say a few words. Anne and Bill used an extension line and would both talk to us. The drill was that we would say 'Hello Mummy, hello Daddy', and they'd ask 'How are you children?'. Each child would have time for a quick reply and would then have to pass the phone on to the next one. We usually got about thirty seconds each. Before we handed the phone on we were expected to say 'I love you' to our parents. Similarly, on the few occasions when we made tapes to send to Anne while she was overseas, there was a rigid order in which we could speak and again we would all be lined up to say 'Hello Mummy and Daddy. I love you'.

When we were older, and if we knew Anne was in Australia, we would sometimes try to telephone her if there was some trouble. She usually stayed at Winberra so it was not too hard, apart from getting access to the phone and risking her wrath if she was not sympathetic to our version of events. The trouble was that Anne tended to believe whoever she spoke to first. So we would always try to get to her first before the Aunties told their side of the story; if she heard it from them, she would not listen to us. It worked sometimes, and we became more adept at getting our own way as we grew older.

In the days at Uptop Anne had blonde, shoulder-length hair, but often wore a blonde wig because her natural hairline was receding (she said her huge forehead denoted spirituality and wisdom). She was a fairly thick-set woman, not very tall – about 158 centimetres – and curvaceous. Later we discovered she went to Hawaii for liposuction and reductive surgery every year. It seems strange, but it was something she told us as we got older. She'd drop hints. She would let slip a remark about needing to have her breasts reduced once more – something like, 'It is nearly time to get my tits done again'. Anne could often be incredibly crude for a woman who presented herself as extremely refined.

Anne was enormously vain. Appearance was all in The Family. Ugly children were treated appallingly, as if they were less worthy. According to ex-cult members, people were even screened by Anne on the basis of their looks when they were trying to join the cult.

As for us, Anne wanted people to believe we were her children, and since she considered herself beautiful it was a certainty that she screened us on our looks, or at least screened our parents. We were to be the ones who would carry on the work of the cult, a direct reflection on her, so she was intensely concerned about our appearance. She used to talk a lot about 'breeding' and about us being from the 'right stock'.

However, sometimes nature plays games. Luke was an absolutely gorgeous child with a cherubic face. But when he reached puberty he became pimply and his hair grew thin and straggly. He's not a bad-looking adult, but nothing compared with what he was like as a child. On his reaching puberty, Anne's treatment of him changed immediately and he went from being the favourite to being reviled.

Anne had an extraordinary number of clothes, a huge range of flowing skirts and blouses, and luxurious silk scarves. They were the finest money could buy, bought on tremendous shopping sprees at Harrods and other exclusive stores in London and Paris. I remember Anne wore a lot of blue. It was her favourite colour. She thought it highlighted her eyes. The bedroom she used at Uptop was crammed with her outfits and jewellery: suits and shoes, diamond and ruby and sapphire rings, ropes of pearls and thick gold chains. Her perfume was by Yves St Laurent. She never let us touch her jewellery but it was clearly expensive – she had a taste for the best things in life.

She also bought some exquisite dresses for us when we were little: identical outfits from Banbury Cross. We had to wear these when she took us to meet people she wanted to impress.

At Broom Farm there was a room full of expensive linen and lace, folded away in obsessive order and never used, just there waiting for the right time. One part of the mansion was particularly grand and richly decorated. The floors were covered with magnificent Persian carpets, the curtains were of the richest velvet, the walls were hung with original paintings and a lot of the furniture and ornaments were antique. Each room had its own colour scheme. There was a Green Room, a Blue Room and a Red Room. We were only allowed in this part of the house on express invitation from Anne.

The huge table in the sumptuous dining-room was laid with real silver cutlery. There were pure silk sheets on Anne's bed. There was a beautiful reception room, lit with chandeliers and furnished with antiques, a huge grand piano and cabinets full of crystal glasses.

In the time that we knew her, Anne was a very rich woman who never denied herself anything. She enjoyed the trappings of her wealth and her power. She more than enjoyed them – they were essential to her.

Judging by all the real estate she owns throughout the world I estimate she is worth at least 150 million dollars. Broom Farm, with its three-storey mansion and 40 hectares or so of farmland, must be worth several million dollars alone. She owns at least one more English house. There is one in Crowborough and, I think, another in Red Hill. She or her companies, Fafette and Audette, owns at least a dozen houses in Ferny Creek and another mansion in Olinda. She and Bill have, or did have a few years ago, a huge property just outside Traralgon. In the United States the large property in the Catskill Mountains outside New York has three houses on it. And of course there was Uptop, 2.5 hectares of waterfront land in a popular holiday area of Lake Eildon.

In contrast to the magnetism of Anne, Bill seemed quite ineffectual. We all knew or had a deep sense that he had no real say.

Even as little kids we realised that the only person we had to get approval from was Anne, and that she was the only person who had the power to change things in our lives. There was something strange and unpredictable about Bill, despite his quiet disposition. It may have been repressed rage against Anne, who so completely dominated him. This feeling seemed to emerge when he was beating us. His beatings were horrible. Bill said he couldn't bear it when we looked surly. He used to accuse us, particularly Andrea and me, of 'dumb insolence' and of a 'bad attitude', and he would punish us for this.

I'll never forget a particular thrashing he gave Andrea. Andrea had been sent by Anne to the upstairs girls' bedroom to get some hair-clips and brushes to do the girls' hair in the downstairs bedroom. Bill passed her on the stairs and said good morning. Andrea didn't respond properly. She just grunted or something. This caused Bill to explode. He grabbed her, and again and again hit her on the head and face, punching her with all his strength, pulling her up when she fell to the ground and hitting her again. When he was finished he threw her against the wall. We could hear him yelling, and we could hear the blows and Andrea's screams from where we stood frozen with terror in the bedroom. We were very scared that his fury was gathering momentum and that he would attack the rest of us as well.

What had Andrea done to deserve this? She'd been in the wrong place at the wrong time, a time when a temporary psychosis overwhelmed his normally timid nature and his anger was deflected onto someone smaller who was not able to defend herself. Perhaps he felt unable or too scared to vent his anger on Anne, the person with whom I think he was probably most angry. I think he secretly hated her for her control of him. He could not cope with the fact that he and everybody else knew that it was Anne who was the master of the household in every conceivable way and he was just a hanger-on, a drone to her queen bee.

Shortly after Bill's explosive beating of Andrea, Anne called all the girls downstairs to the girls' room and attempted to explain

Bill's behaviour; instead she ended up berating us. I would have been 12 or 13 at the time. Anne spoke to us in a crude and almost incomprehensible manner. She said that life all came down to gynaecology. She said she'd been a nurse and she knew a thing or two about loose women. She referred to her time as a matron, when she had allegedly seen prostitutes 'strung up with their legs apart' and great cancers coming out of their genitals 'because they had been such sluts'. She said she had 'smelled enough fannies in her time to know a slut when she met one'.

I was stunned by the language Anne used. She could be absolutely revolting at times and this was one of them. But I was also puzzled about what she was trying to convey. Although she had said that she was going to explain Bill's outburst, she didn't refer at all to the belting incident; nor did she try to excuse Bill or apologise for him. We failed to see how Anne's tirade had any relevance to Bill's being angry with us, but probably to her distorted way of thinking it all made perfect sense.

Even when we were tiny children, the girls would get into trouble for walking in a provocative manner in the presence of male cult members, and be accused of 'waggling' their hips. Often if there was a male guest in the house, Anne made us stay in our rooms while they went to the toilet. We girls were often accused by Anne of 'staring' at men. If we were caught looking directly at them it was somehow supposed to be perverted. When she caught us, or if the men reported us, Anne would punish us and make out that we were sluts. She always used to accuse us of having it off in cubby houses so, whenever we built cubbies she ordered them destroyed as dens of iniquity. She also used to accuse us of masturbating in the shower, which is why showering time was restricted and supervised. If we were caught playing with the boys or in the boys' room at night, we were accused of having a sexual interest in each other. She used to have our underwear inspected, we were never quite sure for what.

Although Anne frequently seemed to be preoccupied with sex, physically she was a fairly cold person. She never let us touch her at all, unless we were invited to give her a kiss or to pose for photographs with her. Even then it was on rare occasions, such as when she came home from overseas, and we were lined up in order of age to give her and Bill a kiss on the cheek.

Nothing was ever spontaneous. It was as if Anne were completely controlling us, never giving us too much of anything: food, affection, warmth, kindness. She managed to keep us always wanting, always longing for her approval. And how desperately we craved it: our whole psyche revolved around the desperate need for her love and attention.

It is very hard to think of Anne with clinical detachment and attempt to understand her as I would a patient of my own. There is too much emotion associated with her, and she is so complex that I find it impossible to categorise her psychiatrically. However, she does exhibit some of the characteristics of psychotic thought disorder: her thoughts skip and derail, she seldom finishes a sentence and she has fantastic and grandiose delusions. But whether the delusions and the disordered and seemingly random thought processes are signs of some mental problem or merely a conscious part of the way she maintains her mystique and power, I don't know. She is such a charismatic figure; so able to convince intelligent people to follow her. She has an intuitive knowledge of human nature and she fudges a lot by not finishing her sentences. A lot of her powerful effect on others is achieved by hinting at things, so that listeners are forced to finish the idea themselves, while believing Anne to possess complete knowledge. She is able to create the illusion that she is privy to higher knowledge and wisdom, which enhances her mystique in the eyes and minds of her followers.

Like Bill, she was prone to violent mood swings when we were children. She would forget what she had said previously, and would deny that she had ever made certain rules or given particular orders. For instance, she once ordered the girls who slept in the downstairs room to swap beds on a fortnightly basis, so that we wouldn't get any ideas that we were superior to anyone else by dint of the fact that some of the beds were higher off the floor than others. Then, a little while later, she threw a tantrum when she found out we weren't sleeping in what she considered to be our normal beds. If we turned around on occasions like this and told her that she herself had given the order for us to change, she flatly denied it – no one was allowed to contradict her.

In early 1993 I spoke to her on the phone and it struck me how oddly she speaks – just like some of the psychotic patients I spoke with when I was on psychiatry rotation during my medical course. I don't think she is overly intelligent but she is incredibly manipulative and completely self-obsessed, as evidenced by her choice of our names – seven were derivatives of the name Anne.

I really do think she has convinced herself of her own version of reality. She probably now genuinely believes her own assertions about how well we were brought up and how much love we were given and how retarded we all were! I think she truly feels that she did love us and look after us and give us a good life, and that she has conveniently forgotten all the cruelties she imposed on us.

Only a few people who invent their own reality are able to get others to believe in it. Starting a socially isolated cult is one way. David Koresh, who was the head of the Branch Davidians in Waco, Texas, was willing to take his life to the brink to prove its reality, but it ultimately meant he had to die to prove that he lived what he believed; to prove himself to himself, his followers and his enemies; to prove, in a distorted sort of way, that what he said was correct.

When Anne Hamilton-Byrne was first challenged in Australia in 1987, after the police rescued us, she could have returned to Australia and stuck by her disciples, if only to prove that she believed what she was preaching. Part of the cult's doctrine is that suffering brings you to a higher level, and therefore closer to God. This indeed was how The Family justified a lot of what they did to us. But when it came to the point of staying and facing the charges, Anne did no such thing. Instead she did not come back, except under police escort a number of years later. Anne, it seems, still has a powerful sense of self-preservation.

Repeatedly we children noticed that there was one set of rules for her and another for her followers. Anne justified the discrepancies in her lifestyle compared with that of her disciples by saying that, because she was an enlightened being, she was on Earth totally out of choice, unlike everyone else who had to be reborn again and again to expiate their karma. She used to say that it was difficult for her to endure being in a physical body because she was divine, and that she went through a lot of suffering in order to be able to stay on Earth and teach her followers. Occasionally she claimed that followers with pride (one of the deadly sins) emitted an odour, imperceptible to normal people but apparent to her more highly developed senses. Of course she declared this odour to be repugnant.

So when I say she may be psychotic, I don't mean I think she's crazy, at least not in the popular conception of the word. What I mean is, I think anyone who has built such a complete fantasy world and been able to sustain it for so long despite the outside reality would be unbalanced. Thirty years of being deferred to as a living deity would upset anyone's equilibrium. As well, everyone she surrounds herself with reinforces her delusions. Because of the number of professional people within the cult, over whom she has complete power, she has been able to manipulate the outside world enough to create the reality she desires.

I have mentioned before that we believed Anne could read our minds, and she constantly told us that she had this power. I can remember a letter from her saying that she hovered above our beds at night in her spirit form and so knew all that was going on and what we were dreaming about. Although it seems incredible now, at the time it did not seem unlikely. We believed that, as children, we were at the lowest end of the pecking order, that everyone else had more power than us, so we believed everything we were told. Looking back I can see what Anne was doing, but then I had no idea.

We'd be in meditation and she'd be leading us and she'd say,

'Right, I know you're not concentrating. You're thinking about your next feed'. When you consider the pathetic amounts of food they gave us, it wouldn't be hard for an adult to assume that we were thinking about our next feed, but to us it seemed that Anne did have some extraordinary power. During meditation she would claim to be able to 'tune in' to each one of us by turn, in an effort, she maintained, to keep our thoughts strictly spiritual and acceptable to her.

I always expected to be hit by a bolt of lightning when my thoughts wandered off the subject of Christ or the Buddha or whoever else we were supposed to be worshipping at the time. Sometimes I would be day-dreaming about what we were going to have for tea and I'd catch myself and pray that she hadn't picked up my thoughts. The notion that she could read minds, a notion unquestioned by adult cult members and children alike, reinforced the concept that she was a direct representative of God.

It is difficult to say now whether Anne had any good qualities. I remember once when I was being beaten by Bill and I looked at her and she told him to stop it. Maybe I looked particularly pleading, maybe she didn't have the stomach for it that day, who knows? But that was one time when she showed some humanity. I remembered and clung to that act of compassion and took it to mean that I meant something to her; but looking back now that seems silly because it was she who had initiated the belting in the first place.

Often we didn't comprehend that Anne was behind our treatment so we blamed the Aunties instead. I think that, too, was part of the design. If we had been capable of analysing our situation more fully we probably would have realised Anne's dominant role in all this, but it was far easier to use the Aunties as a scapegoat instead of ruining our fantasy of a loving and kind mother.

Sometimes Anne would look at us in a way that convinced us that she really did love us. I don't know. It's hard to convey just how devoted we were to her and how much importance we placed on her every look and thought that related to us. We wanted so much for her to love us. It hurts me inside thinking of how much I wanted her love. But I don't think she ever did love us.

She lived in, and created for us, a world of deceptions, lies and inconsistencies. The legacy of this continues today in all of us: at times we experience a feeling of worthlessness, a conviction of being innately unworthy, a sense of being powerless to affect what is happening to us. By her control over the spiritual aspects of our lives, by her subjugation of us by physical means, and by her constant assault on our belief in our own worth, Anne was able to systematically break down our sense of self. This, and the constant cruelty she displayed towards us, led us to lose our trust in ourselves and others, to feel a pervading sense of guilt and to accept willingly the blame for everything that went wrong.

Nobody ever allowed us the basic rights that all children should have – to be loved and to have someone to trust. Anne deliberately set out to turn us into adults who couldn't form emotional attachments to anyone but herself. None of the Aunties was allowed to give us presents or show affection towards us or to touch us physically, apart from when they belted us. She wanted us to be unable to cope in the outside world so we would be forced to remain dependent on her. I really don't think she is capable of love or affection for anyone; I don't see how she can be, given the things she has done to us and continues to do to others.

CHAPTER 9

The world according to Anne

The basis of The Family's religion was that Anne was a living deity and the reincarnation of Jesus Christ. The cult's doctrine said Jesus Christ was a great master who came down to earth, but that he wasn't the only one; Buddha and Krishna were other enlightened beings who came to us. Anne was placed in the same category.

The rest of the cult's beliefs were a hotch-potch of Christianity and Eastern mysticism. Most of the teachings revolved around the virtue of suffering: how beneficial it was to the soul and how it had to be embraced as the path to enlightenment. A lot of emphasis was placed on austerity, chastity, meditation and silence.

As children, our beliefs were fairly loose and determined by Anne. Mostly we read the great Hindu scriptures, and we studied some Buddhist and Zen philosophy as well. We were taught the concepts of karma and reincarnation and the attainment of self-realisation through spiritual work, beliefs that form some of the fundamental tenets of Eastern religious philosophy. At Christmas and Easter we concentrated on the Bible.

Some of the cult's beliefs dictated by Anne were, however, a little more radical. For example, Anne decreed that Hell was not hot but cold, and one of her methods of getting back at someone who had displeased her was to write the name of the wrongdoer on a piece of paper and put it in the freezer under an ice cube – thereby consigning that person to Hell. Alternatively, she would stick pins in wax dolls to cause discomfort and illness in people she thought had done her wrong. Even more heretical to followers of Christianity, Anne insisted that all cult members perform the sign of the cross in the opposite direction to that prescribed by the Church. She also claimed that the end of the world was imminent and that only those who were living in the Dandenongs would survive.

Every Thursday night, and on Sunday nights as well when Anne was in the country, the disciples of the cult would gather at Santiniketan Lodge in Ferny Creek, opposite Raynor Johnson's house. Anne also had another hall in the hills called the White Lodge, but this was for smaller meetings of inner core members, more intimate meditation and discussion, and LSD sessions. Santiniketan was built like a church, except it had lush, dark blue velvet carpet, and an extremely good sound and heating system. The hall was furnished with rows of chairs that could seat a couple of hundred people. The building also contained a library and a sound room where all Anne's talks were recorded.

In the hall about 3 metres separated the front row of seats from several carpeted steps that led up to Anne's throne-like chair and the little reading table where she sat to deliver her sermons. Behind this was a large altar over which hung a gigantic image of the crucifixion. On the altar were many of the symbols of various religions: a number of Jewish menorahs, a statue of the Buddha, and several symbols of the Hindu faith, including a representation of the word 'Om'. There was an elaborate lighting system. In contrast to the body of the hall, which was in darkness, Anne was surrounded by a bluish light that created an aura around her. A light, too, fell on the crucifix, but the rest of the hall was shrouded in darkness.

All the initiated disciples – about 150 people – were expected to attend the Thursday night sermons whether Anne was present or not. Not to come was considered defiance, and people would be censured for their absence by other members or by Anne herself. When Anne was not there, members would listen to tapes of her earlier talks. On the nights Anne was present, the whole cult would gather and meditate for about an hour in the darkened hall. Incense would be burning and soft music playing, and I remember the room was always extremely hot and stuffy. Then the background music would stop, replaced by the strains of Handel's 'Largo' from *Xerxes*, and the blue light would pick out Anne as she walked down the aisle between the rows of chairs: all the disciples would stand as she entered. She would take her seat before the altar and everyone would kneel on the floor until the music had finished. Anne would then usually say, 'Good evening, my brethren' or 'Hello, my friends'. No one else was allowed to talk, although sometimes she would ask if specific people were in attendance and they would acknowledge their presence.

Next, Anne led members in the Lord's Prayer. They would all kneel for this, then recite the special mantra of the cult:

To thy last supper
Let me be allowed to stay
O Son of God
For neither have I betrayed any secrets to thine enemies
Nor have I given thee a kiss of Judas
But like a thief, I pray unto thee
Remember me O Lord
As I enter into Thy glorious Kingdom
Almighty God.

This was considered an intensely secret and powerful mantra. Many of the words held special importance, and were given special emphasis, and also reiterated when one was 'going-through'. It has taken me seven years to be able to recite this mantra without fear of retribution. Even now as I write it my heart is pounding and I am filled with a nameless anxiety.

After the recitation Anne would continue to pray in soliloquy, asking for special blessings for those who were ill, for those who were having any crises of faith. It was often during these prayers that she would recall those whom she had singled out earlier, and make it clear to everyone that they had done something wrong. She would accuse them, in this public forum, of not trusting enough or suffering enough to justify being on the true path, or of not being true enough disciples, or of not living up to their initiation vows. Or she would simply say that she was disappointed with several people – they knew who they were. Everyone would be cringing at this point, hoping that they would not be singled out for her displeasure.

A typical sermon from Anne on a Thursday night would be preceded by music: Handel's *Messiah*, Beethoven's Ninth, a theme by Albinoni, or the signature song of the cult, Handel's 'Largo'. Then she would answer letters from those in the cult who had written to her about their earthly or spiritual troubles during the preceding week. I have a tape of one of Anne's Thursday night sermons in which she answered some of these letters. I will quote directly from it to illustrate how she rambles and how often what she says is either incomprehensible or ambiguous. Referring to a particular letter, she said:

> Not being able to accept or understand what's going on in your life and you're initiated too, do you think it should be easier? Many, many down the ages have wondered why life seems to hit back in a much stronger way when one is initiated or is it just you, you say. It happens on all paths of truth my friend, many amongst us everywhere can see a pattern through the pain and the suffering in the world and in ourselves. And even though you've been on the path of the light for twenty years or more as soon as the pattern shows up or you see through it. The initiated soul is at a stage of a strong inner conviction that he or she is now able to see the light at the end of the tunnel. If not all the time, some of the time. When that happens there isn't a lot of time to waste for the spiritual quickening will take place.

Our body, our nerve system, our brain, our pulses will all work towards this great, mighty issue of our soul. Don't waste time in being anxious. By the time you get to this stage you laugh at anyone who judges others, but don't even judge them, don't laugh at anyone who judges others, there's no judgement left if you've reached that stage. One of the main things in that learning is don't put yourself in the position or anyone else, to be in the shadow of your judge or their judgement or self-appointed ideas or thoughts. Even if you are at the fundamental beginning of the path of that spiritual training you are aware of strengths that will come to you through initiation, and then of course there is the meditation, which is the gate that has to open all other levels of consciousness.

She would continue on in that vein; the tape I have goes for forty-five minutes and doesn't get any more intelligible than the above words. The disciples in front would be listening intently for a personal message, and struggling to attribute a meaning to what was essentially continuous free association and raving.

Next we would say further prayers, including the Lord's Prayer again, and listen to some more music. Anne would preach a second sermon for about an hour; generally she would read from written notes, which often contained a lot of direct quotations from the scriptures of other religions. In later years I knew her teachings were rarely original because I would find great slabs of what she had said in the religious books of writers and teachers such as Meher Baba. In fact, often the only time her talks made any sense was when she was quoting from someone else. Once when we confronted one of the Aunties about this they became very defensive, saying the other master must have copied from Anne, and not vice versa.

After the reading, Anne would free associate. She would berate certain members of the cult, talk about being persecuted, give special messages to some disciples and lead prayers for others. A number of collection plates were placed near the door and everyone would be expected to give donations in the form of a cheque or an envelope full of money – not just in one plate but in all of them. Each plate supposedly represented a different charity – one or two were even for the animals.

Who were the disciples of the cult? Who were those people who sat in that hall every Thursday night and listened, enraptured, to Anne's teachings, and whose lives were lived in poverty, austerity and misery due to her teachings of self-denial? We children had no choice about belonging to this group, but who were the adults from the outside world who submitted themselves without question to a set of bizarre expectations and beliefs?

I believe three groups of people made up the cult. The first group I consider to be the innocents, the true believers; the second group are the brain-washed followers who have given up thinking for themselves; the last group, made up of people who form the inner core of the cult, I think of as evil. I see them as no more than criminals out for all the cult can offer them.

Anne had complete control of the lives of all cult members. They relied on her to make even the smallest decision and cult doctrine reinforces this. Providing they stayed in favour with the Master – and that was the definition of a good disciple – she would assume responsibility for them for all the years to come. The Master assumed karmic responsibility for all past actions of a new disciple upon initiation into the cult. The slate was wiped clean. If you were an innocent looking for a God on Earth, this must have sounded pretty good.

Anyone who started to question Anne's wisdom or power was told that his or her intellect was a handicap to spiritual enlightenment. Contradictions in Anne's teachings or actions were explained away as demonstrations of the uncleanliness of mind of less spiritual beings, and you were made to feel deeply guilty for asking any questions. You were not allowed to ask what she meant when she didn't make sense: you were supposed to meditate and ponder on her words and when you were spiritual enough the meaning of the message would become clear.

We believed, and in fact had witnessed, that the Master's wrath could be terrifying if she was deceived, crossed or disobeyed. We did not question that her displeasure could manifest itself in physical or psychological injury, causing the believer to contract cancer or to lose a loved one through an accident. A rational person accepts the inevitability of such things in life, but when they occurred in cult members' lives they were tied into the belief system and used to reinforce Anne's powers.

Provided believers were complete in their faith – that is, had no doubts and worshipped Anne wholeheartedly – they were able to ignore all previously held morality. They could justify any action because, they reasoned, if the Master told them to do it, it must be all right. Anne's teaching was that earthly morality was quite different from spiritual morality. So there she was, giving people permission to do anything, as long as they did what she told them and believed in her completely.

This was the 1960s and Anne was saying that anything went as long as she said so. That meant sex, drugs and power. It was a tempting combination for many of Melbourne's professionals. Anne gave them permission to ignore all the rules of society. They were special, they belonged to Anne, and that meant they were obeying a higher law than the laws governing ordinary people. These people relinquished all conscience and responsibility for their actions to Anne and in fact became almost willing slaves to her.

I remember a dinner table conversation a number of years ago when Anne was holding forth on one of her theories. She said Earth was hollow and aliens lived in the centre of it. I didn't say anything at the time about the aliens but I knew she was talking utter rubbish. Some of her assumptions about geography and geology were so wrong I felt compelled, even though silently, to challenge them. There must have been others at the table who knew she was raving. Most of them were educated people, but not one of them said anything. I think if she had said 'The world is made of green cheese' even the most intellectual among them would have agreed.

She often used to say that she was 'twenty or thirty years ahead of what scientists had discovered', and so lots of her more extreme statements were accepted by cult members as truths that science had not yet uncovered. Anne believed that she had access to knowledge only possessed by spirits on another plane and that this knowledge would only be revealed to scientists when the spirits believed that humanity was ready to use it properly.

It is very difficult to explain why the core cult members, those who knew most about Anne, adhered to her bizarre beliefs. In comparison with her, many must have been of superior intellect and almost all were better educated. She had no formal qualifications other than those she dreamed up, and she was a plagiarist. Surely some of these people should have been clever enough to look beyond the veneer of spirituality and see the hypocrisy of preaching asceticism while living in self-indulgent luxury? But one runs up against a strange dichotomy when one examines the cult leaders and those who followed them. I cannot comprehend how these educated people couldn't see through Anne.

The bulk of the cult was made up of professional people. Without their support and participation, Anne Hamilton-Byrne would never have become what she is today. It was their names, or more importantly, the letters that went after their names, that gave her the credibility and social power she needed – which in turn gave her the means to keep those she already had and to recruit more and similar people into the cult. These professional people – doctors, lawyers, engineers, architects, psychiatrists, nurses and social workers – allowed her successfully to pull the wool over everyone's eyes for more than twenty years.

Had The Family been a group of strangely dressed people meeting once or twice a week for meditation, an address by a Master, and chanting and the playing of music, they would never have gone unnoticed for so long. But professionals in their pin-striped conservative suits, and with their impeccable social credentials, could get away with maintaining morals in their private life that were completely at variance with their professional ethics. They looked respectable, therefore people thought they must be respectable.

Who were these professionals? They were doctors who wrote out the prescriptions that controlled us and other cult members; lawyers who wrote out the deed polls that were needed to forge the passports and birth certificates that created our false identities; social workers who allowed Anne to bypass normal channels to adopt or, in some instances, simply steal, so many children; nurses who gave her contacts with dying rich people who then left their estates to her; doctors who treated those same rich people and signed their death certificates; psychiatrists who had people committed to Newhaven Hospital; and doctors and nurses who supervised the abuse of LSD (which for a while the doctors actually obtained free of charge from the Swiss drug company Sandoz, in return for research information). Without drugs Anne's power would have been diminished enormously.

No one questioned Anne, and the children at Uptop bore the brunt of all the secrecy. We were her victims. Yet so, too, were the adults who failed to take, or were incapable of applying, any sort of intellectual approach to what Anne said. Nothing added up and yet none of them questioned, or thought for themselves, or attempted to test the truth of what she was saying.

To leave a cult like this takes massive courage. On Anne's orders these people had cut ties with their own families of origin unless they too were cult members. Their social and professional circles mostly consisted of cult people. If cult members showed any kind of doubt they were persecuted by everyone they knew. Vicious rumours began and, however improbable the rumours seemed, the victims were ostracised, condemned, threatened – sometimes physically – and made to feel like a miserable Judas for doubting the Master. However, if they recanted, they were once more accepted into the cult with open arms. Many of the professionals in The Family had broken the law for Anne and they knew how easy it would be for Anne to see to it that they lost their jobs and their reputations. So it was in their interests to stay safe and silent within the bosom of The Family.

And then there were the inner core members: the evil ones. I believe that they were only in for what they could get. They were under no delusions about Anne's holiness; they stayed because it suited them. Their motivation was simply the quest for power. M. Scott Peck in his book *People of the Lie* describes the evil personality as someone who seeks power over others, who has a need to subjugate life and liveliness in others, and who possesses a total lack of insight into the enormity of his or her own wrongdoings. These people are recognisable by the number and complexity of their lies.

The snobbery and elitism that existed among the inner core members illustrates this. The more they got away with, the more they felt superior to the rest of society, and the more confident they became in following the path of evil. The guilt of these people is unquestionable: they established the cult, they targeted patients and friends, they administered drugs, they ran Newhaven, they falsified documents, and they carried out Anne's dirty work. They dealt with the huge inflows and outflows of money that Anne commanded. And because there were only ten or twelve of them, they even rationalised their behaviour by claiming to be the reincarnations of Christ's apostles, working towards some great unseen spiritual goal. They will remain with Anne to the end. Each has multiple names and identities, and their legacy is a farrago of lies.

I think one reason Anne remained unchallenged for so long has to do with The Family's recruitment methods, which were simple and almost unvaried. Often the people recommended to Anne held the same sorts of jobs as those doing the recommending. I've often wondered why these highly intelligent people, the so-called cream of society, should have been so vulnerable. I have reached certain conclusions about this, although I have no evidence to back them up. Despite their apparent worldly success, these people were unhappy. They were looking for something more. They felt failures on a personal and spiritual plane. They wanted someone to lead them, someone to guide them in making decisions about their lives, someone they could surrender totally to on all levels. They could not handle the existential loneliness of being a human being. Many of them had unhappy family lives, or had suffered abuse as children. Some simply had psychiatric problems and were looking for a cure. Enter Anne Hamilton-Byrne. Anne was like a spider spinning a web. Single lonely people, often newly divorced or separated, were her prey. She sought them out. Information about people with emotional problems came her way through her spies in the medical profession. Entrapment began gently.

Someone in the cult would tell Anne about a friend or an acquaintance who was unhappy, questioning his or her existence or just going through a difficult period of life. The person's child may have just died or, more commonly, his or her marriage may have broken up, though frequently it was something much less serious. Some of Anne's victims were just having a mid-life crisis. Anne got all the private details. It didn't matter if the person was a patient of a doctor or a nurse in The Family, because professional confidentiality meant nothing to the cult.

Once the candidate was chosen, a 'softening-up' process began in which the cult member opened the person's mind to the possibility of seeking alternative rather than conventional help. The cult member might suggest the person see a 'very wise lady' who in the past had helped others enormously with their problems. Alternatively, the cult member might recommend that the candidate go to a prayer meeting on the grounds that the spiritual side of life is so comforting and that the cult member had derived so much from these meetings. The vulnerable person had no reason not to trust the friend, or the doctor or psychiatrist – another advantage of having professionals as recruitment officers.

Trusting the cult member, the candidate went along to the meeting, which would not seem particularly bizarre, and afterwards would be introduced to Anne. She mysteriously seemed to know every detail about the candidate, and showered him or her with attention and charm, and everyone around her made the person feel special and welcome. It was not long before the person received an invitation to be given the 'opportunity of a religious experience'. There was no mention that LSD would play a part in this experience.

When the cult controlled Newhaven Hospital, things were very easy. Potential cult members were booked into Newhaven and, once there, were completely at Anne's mercy. Her psychiatrists would put them under LSD for days, even up to a week. They would be left alone in dark rooms while under the influence of the drug and every now and then there would be visitations by Anne herself. During these 'go-throughs' or 'clearings', in the parlance of the cult, you were supposed to 'look at yourself' and see how horrible you were, and expected to confess to incidents you were ashamed of in the past or to secret fears or hang-ups. You were supposed to be able to abreact – relive past experiences – so that these things could be put behind you and resolved. Sometimes Anne targeted special qualities, which she called 'blocks' (to enlightenment), which you were supposed to 'look at' and 'work on' while under the influence of the drug. While at first LSD was probably used openly in the hospital by cult psychiatrists, after it became illegal it was still used – and continues to be – by Anne, as a form of seeking and maintaining mind control. The hallucinatory effects of the drug were well exploited. If you didn't have a guilt complex or a hang-up before you went through, you were sure to have one by the time they had finished with you. Sexual hang-ups were a cult speciality. Through your drug-induced haze Anne appeared God-like – she even said she was Jesus Christ – and you realised she offered you a way to attain the true potential of your spirituality. You would repent of the things you had confessed and realise that only through Anne could you ever expect redemption.

After a couple of sessions people were usually converted. It is interesting that most of the professionals in The Family have been in it since it began and those who have left tended to do so right at the start. There are no in-betweens in The Family.

Anne used what was said to her during these 'go-throughs' as a means of controlling members for the rest of their lives, and as time passed she exerted more and more control. If any members finally saw through the veneer and realised what a hypocrite she was, they could not leave. Compromised completely, they stood to lose everything by leaving. This is a real situation for many people.

Or was it just the charisma of the woman that kept members in thrall? Believe me, Anne has plenty of it. And it wasn't just the children who felt it. Looking through newspaper files on The Family is a revelation. For example, in an article in the *Australian Women's Weekly* in October 1987, a former cult member, known as Elizabeth, recalled Anne as being 'incredibly loving at first ... But if you failed at anything then the tongue-lashings would begin'. Elizabeth said her children were taken from her and given to other cult members:

> She parted people from their children because she wouldn't have complete control over people if they were still making decisions about their children. We were told the children would be brought up away from outside influences by people who'd looked after them in previous lives ... It's hard to understand how so many educated and privileged people could become ensnared. What you have to understand is the power of the woman's personality. She played God and we – stupidly – accepted her decisions. We rationalised that she had to know best ... If anyone resisted too hard, there were always doctors to administer drugs.

In the *Age* in September 1983 David Elias wrote at length about Anne's methods and about Newhaven Hospital. Elias was contacted by George, a former patient, whose case perfectly illustrates the way the hospital was run.

In 1966 George was a patient at Newhaven, being treated for alcoholism. He had been a medical student at Queen's College at Melbourne University when Doctor Raynor Johnson was still Master there. Doctor Johnson visited a patient in the next bed and he recognised George. Another frequent visitor of George was

Anne Hamilton-Byrne, who was then Mrs Riley. 'This was to be the lady who captivated me with her talk of spiritual things, her knowledge of God and a familiarity with things psychic and her soothsaying', he told Elias, adding that 'even then she had a sort of charisma'. She suggested to George that, on his discharge from Newhaven, it would be disastrous to return to his solitary life in his flat and that instead he should stay with her at her home in Ferny Creek.

As a consequence George went to live with Anne and soon found he was being 'introduced to the mysteries of the procedures of the cult'. He was initiated into The Family and later married another member – at Anne's suggestion – although that marriage has since broken down.

George detailed his attendances at clearings where cult members were given drugs under the supervision of three psychiatrists. He claimed the clearings were carried out at Newhaven and in private houses. Sometimes as many as six cult members would be going-through at one time. He talked about Anne's method, which involved having cult members sit with those going-through and reporting back to her on anything that was said. Anne then used this knowledge to create the impression that she had psychic powers.

George and his family were sent to England several times and once to India by Anne. Later Anne sent him to Uptop as a cook and to look after us.

George talked about how he and other cult members had nursed Lord Casey, after a serious road accident. He was assigned to watch over Lord Casey at night and to give him his medication. All this despite the fact that he had only ever had a small amount of training as a medical student.

From accounts like this it is possible to gain some insight into how Anne attained her power. All those who came under her spell acknowledge her extraordinary charisma. Still, the truth is, she wouldn't have been half as successful without the support of someone as eminent as Doctor Raynor Johnson.

Raynor Johnson wrote a little paper for Anne in the 1960s, which was a blueprint for the Kai Lama experiment. It contained a biography of the Master and praised her wisdom. I know it quite well because in a fit of do-gooding I typed it out. There is a section in it called 'Suffer the Little Children to Come Unto Me'. Doctor Raynor Johnson wrote:

This is perhaps the most amazing aspect of my Master's work. Viewed as a piece of organisation with devoted and sacrificial help, it is staggering in its outlook, yet it was planned with a consciousness of its magnitude and the great responsibility of this undertaking. It had to cover 10 to 15 years before it could lead to success. Only a great Master, equally at home in this world and the next, could have hoped to carry it through to a conclusion.

It amounted to this – a group of children, some already born here, some yet to be born, were brought together, fostered and adopted and trained from the beginning of their lives in as perfect conditions as could be provided. Their health was meticulously supervised and *all* aspects of their welfare and education were considered and provided for. Before they came it was known by the Master when and where and to what parents they were coming and what qualities potentially they brought with them from past lives.

It is safe to say the future age will see them, unknown though they are, as custodians and continuers of the work their Master has set going in many parts of the world.

CHAPTER 10

Initiation into The Family

My memory of being initiated into the cult is inextricably bound up with my memory of a particularly bad crime I committed in about 1984, when I was almost fourteen. Although, by definition, we were members of the cult because we were Anne's children, we were not yet initiated into all the mysteries.

The events leading up to my terrible crime began when I started taking midnight walks with Annette. We were taking a huge chance wandering around outside the property in the middle of the night but we thought we could get away with it. And so, late at night when everything was quiet, Annette and I would sneak out for a bit of adventure. We planned these escapades well and no one else knew what we were doing. Annette even made some moccasins out of some old fabric so we could creep out on the gravel path without being heard, though I reckoned I didn't need them as I knew that yard so well.

At first we stayed just within the yard, not doing anything much except enjoying the sensations of danger and naughtiness. Then gradually we ventured further and further away. Getting outside the property caused a massive adrenaline rush. Going outside the gates was pure defiance – in fact it was the biggest crime we could have committed.

We were filled with trepidation at our temerity and with the danger of what we were doing. We must have known that we would get caught eventually, that it was just a matter of time. And yet we couldn't have stopped. We were tasting adventure and excitement and we felt daring and free at night as we never could during the cold, rigid day at Uptop.

We ranged further and further afield, exploring the neighbouring houses and properties. One night we discovered that one of the windows was broken in a house not far down the road from Uptop, so we decided to explore.

Annette did not dare go in at first, but once I had reported what was inside she overcame her fear. Much to our delight we saw that the fridge in the house was well stocked. We thought we were in Heaven – unlimited access to food was possible! One of the first things we ate was a frozen pizza-sub, raw, which at the time I thought was exquisite, although now the thought of it makes me sick.

I suppose it was inevitable that some of the other kids found out and insisted on coming. Things started to get out of hand. We found another house, closer to us, with its verandah door open, and we ventured inside. Luke got carried away and started pinching things other than food. On one occasion he stole a bundle of hay for a cubby – a rather large item that was difficult to conceal.

That was the beginning of the end. More and more kids became involved, which was bound to happen when you think about how little adventure we experienced in our lives. This was the biggest thing we kids had ever dared to do and the excitement was palpable. Eventually Luke had a small gang operating independently and I didn't know what they were doing. I tried to stop them because I could see that it was getting out of control and that discovery and disaster must surely follow. But it was already too late. Luke promised me he would stop but the very next day Aunty Margy caught him and a few others at the house closest to Uptop.

Getting caught changed the way things were forever. We had never been so bad before and we knew it. Everything for which we had ever been punished paled into insignificance in comparison.

We walked around in a daze, and a terrified sense of impending doom descended on the house. We could not even begin to guess at what they'd do to us. What could be worse than what they'd meted out already?

To begin with, the Aunties gave us the silent treatment. They sent us to Coventry as traitors, and those of us who were the main culprits were treated as the lowest form of life. We were called Judases, and accused of the worst crime in the cult: betraying Anne, the divine Master. Interrogations began, led by Uncle Leon. Each child was questioned separately about his or her involvement, except me because they reckoned I was the ring-leader. The other kids were coerced by the Aunties into informing on me. They behaved like spies, making up what they didn't know rather than risk sharing my punishment.

I'd already decided to take sole responsibility and accept the punishment. After all I had started it and had done the lion's share of the food stealing, and I didn't believe in dobbing in the others. But I was surprised by the way the other kids turned against me. Some of the boys blamed everything on me. I took it without complaint although I was inwardly devastated and very hurt by the boys' cowardice. I knew that they were scared, but I expected them to at least take a little of the blame for what they had done. Although I had started it, I'd only taken food whereas Luke had taken things like a clock radio and hay, which I thought was more serious than stealing food. But in the end I got the blame for everything. It took me a long time to get over that part of it, to understand the fear that must have motivated my brothers and sisters. I felt completely alone, and alone I had to face the wrath of Anne and Bill.

This was the first time I'd ever felt isolated from the other kids. I had been segregated from them by my actions, but I also felt they lost integrity by not supporting me. I knew I'd done the wrong thing but at least I was willing to face up to my part in it. It took a few years to get over the feeling of separation and of betrayal and to forgive and forget the other children's mixed-up emotions of that time.

Initiation into The Family

Anne and Bill were on the point of returning from overseas when we were found out and I had to await their arrival before punishment was administered. They had been overseas for more than a year at this stage and we were missing them badly. Each time we had been naughty they had put off their homecoming, declaring that they couldn't come home due to our bad behaviour: they were too disappointed in us to make the effort. Before they arrived home this time they sent a few advance salvos. They said they didn't ever really want to see us again; that they disowned us as their children; that we were gutter scum; that we made them sick. They would, however, come up and give me my punishment and punish anyone else who deserved it. They said that we were Judases and that they would gladly trade us in for adopted Indian children who, they argued, would be grateful instead of so wicked.

The Aunties barely fed us during those terrible days when we waited for Anne and Bill to come home. Trish would bash me every now and again, drag me around by the hair and hit me. I pretended I could take it, that I was a tough cookie who didn't care, and that I wasn't sorry for what I'd done. Then something in me snapped and I told Trish she wasn't going to belt me any more. I told her I would wait for punishment from my parents and from them alone. The next time she grabbed me by the hair and started to drag me off the bed, I twisted around and kicked her as hard as I could in the face. I drew blood from her lip.

After that I was treated as a dangerous animal and the other kids were told not to go near me. They were supposed to turn their faces away when they saw me. They were not allowed to talk to me at all. At that stage I did not want any of them near me anyway.

Finally the day of reckoning dawned. Anne and Bill arrived and the tension that had been gathering reached a climax. We were all called upstairs and asked why we had committed such crimes and whether we had anything to say for ourselves. One of my sisters recalls how she dearly wanted to scream in reply, 'Because we wanted you to notice us! We wanted to bring you home!' But she was too scared and knew well that it would have been pointless:

they would never have made the effort to understand us.

I stepped forward. 'I did it', I said, 'no one else was involved.' I was trying to act tough and as if I didn't care about what would happen next. But I was shaking.

Anne told me to come over to where she was seated on the pouffe. She took her red high-heeled shoe off and started belting me with the heel of it. Someone threw me to the ground and told me to take my pants off but I wouldn't. Whatever happened, I was determined not to take my pants down and not to cry.

Anne must have tired herself out because Bill took over. He concentrated on hitting me around the head. I started yelling despite myself. He banged my head against the floor and I still remember seeing stars. I remember that this amazed me because I thought it was just something that happened in fiction. I fought to stay conscious because I thought if I passed out they would have won. I vaguely remember the other kids being huddled in a group and that they looked frightened.

It ended. They kicked me downstairs to bed. I was desperate that the others didn't come near me. I put my face into my pillow. I was all right on my own, but if someone had said anything to me I would have lost it. I cried inside. I felt completely alone, but I think in a way that belting taught me how to survive on my own.

It wasn't long after this that I was formally initiated into the cult, with my brothers Luke and Timothy (it had just been disclosed that we were triplets). I don't know why they chose this time for my initiation. I suppose the 'houses incident' had made them think I was becoming unruly, as we all were, and that it was time to bring me back under Anne's strict control. It was about August 1984 and was just before the boys were due to go overseas to an English boarding school called Stoneyhurst. The boys were provided with false school reports written by Helen Buchanan and Leon Dawes on Aquinel College letterhead paper that had been specially printed for the occasion.

For a few weeks before the initiation we had to read a book called *Yoga and the Bible*. This was supposed to teach us how a newly initiated cult member was meant to behave. The initiation ceremonies were always held on a Sunday evening at Santiniketan Lodge and every member of the cult was supposed to attend as a mark of respect for the Master.

In itself it was not a difficult ceremony, being initiated into The Family. It mainly involved declaring loyalty to Anne; swearing allegiance to the Master. It was the implications of the ceremony that were difficult, for now we were expected to act as disciples and not just as children. We were expected to fulfil our spiritual responsibilities as well as our earthly ones.

The benefits of initiation were all-encompassing; now you had the one true Master as your guru so the attainment of Nirvana was possible in this lifetime. You no longer had to wait for millions of incarnations to work your way to enlightenment like all the other ordinary people. However, because on initiation the Master took on your karmic debt and you started with a clear slate, it was up to you after that to score high on good karma and collect no more of the bad sort – this view of Anne's was a very dualistic and simplistic understanding of the complexities of karma.

Much was made of the fact that Timothy, Luke and I were the youngest-ever initiates of The Family. I didn't really want to be initiated but at the same time I suppose I was flattered by the assumption that this was an immense honour being accorded me, that I was finally deemed worthy enough to become an Initiate of the Path. This was part of Anne's technique for control. Although at times she could make you feel you were beneath contempt, she could, on the other hand, make you feel special, marked just by knowing her. To be her children gave us real status within The Family, on a spiritual as well as a social level.

The reason why I did not want to become an initiate of The Family was because I was having doubts about Anne and the cult. The hypocrisy of a brotherhood that preached love and respect and kindness, and yet was made up of members who treated each other as they did, was beginning to get to me. Also I knew that, once initiated, I was meant to believe that Anne was perfect, since perfection is a prerequisite for gurus. Gurus are meant to be able to emerge spotless from any scrutiny of their character and actions by their disciples. Yet I had started to see Anne as failing me as a mother, which meant, if I didn't think she was good enough to be my mother, she couldn't be my guru.

It was all very complicated at the time. To fully explain it I would have to go back a few years, to the time after we returned from our trip to the United States where we had seen a lot of Baba Muktananda. I had a great devotion to him at this time, and during the long months when Andrea and I had to endure separation as a punishment, I spent a lot of time reading his books, meditating, chanting the Sri Guru Gita, and doing japa (repetition of a mantra on a string of rudrashka beads, which I did with a string, called a mala, that Baba had given me as a gift when I was eight). When I wasn't doing formal japa, I repeated the mantra all the time, with every step that I took inside and outside the house. Andrea and I would stay awake at night until after the Aunties had gone to bed and the house was all quiet, then sneak a meeting with each other in the bathroom, where one of us had to sleep, so that we could chant the Sri Guru Gita in an all-night session. During that dreadful time, these practices were comforting because I believed that, so long as I continued them, Baba would be, on a spiritual level, looking after me. They helped me to cope, psychologically and physically, with the hardship of our punishment and with the abandonment by Anne at that time. I reassured myself that Baba, at least, cared for me, even though my world was pretty bleak. I became intensely religious in my devotion to Baba, and that gave me the strength to endure the punishments with equanimity.

My feelings for Baba continued even after his death in October 1982. Anne did not tell us that Baba had died – or attained Mahasamadhi – until a phone conversation in mid-1983. I cannot begin to explain just how much his death affected me – the utter devastation I experienced. My world crumbled and I felt lost and abandoned on a spiritual level. My belief in him and love for him had seen me through the bad times of my life and now there was nothing left to believe in, no guru figure to worship and follow. Anne and The Family were the only alternative.

As I approached initiation in 1984 I knew I wasn't ready because, although Baba was dead, it somehow felt unfaithful to be swapping him for Anne. Thus my predicament. I felt ambivalent about accepting Anne as my guru when I considered Baba to hold this position. I knew you could not have two gurus. I felt a loyalty to him because my faith in him had sustained me through the bad times in my youth, and also because I sincerely believed him to be perfect and I respected him. However, once again my life was being controlled by others, and I was not allowed to have any say in the choice of who was to be my Master. Anne expected me to become an initiate of her Family and that was all there was to it. And after initiation, going-through would follow. Going-through meant LSD trips. Everyone knew that it was the inevitable consequence of initiation, that it was one of the rituals integral to the spiritual development of the new initiate.

After initiation my psychological turmoil remained. Here I was, I'd just been initiated and I didn't even have a real faith in my new guru, who was also my mother.

The confusion in my life was made worse by what was happening to my body. I had just reached puberty but I had no idea what was happening to me. When I got my first period I thought that I had cut my leg. Then when I washed my leg and saw there was no cut there, I went to see Aunty Christabel. She wasn't very interested in my plight; she just gave me some pads to wear (they were the old-fashioned sort that had to be held in place with a special elastic belt), said I wasn't sick and seemed a bit revolted by me. It wasn't until I was doing Year Twelve biology that I worked out the meaning of menstruation. At 14 (although I was really 16), I just took it as further evidence of how disgusting I really was.

All these new things that were happening were forcing me to become an adult. The imminent ritual of going-through would give me the chance to enter the magical world of the grown-up, to become something more than a sub-human child. In that winter of 1984, when I left my childhood behind on the secluded shores of Lake Eildon and arrived at Broom Farm in England, I did not feel nearly ready to join this world.

CHAPTER 11

Going-through

Shortly before my initiation Anne changed my name and gave me a new identity. No longer was I to be called Andrée, who allegedly had been born in June, July or September 1970. Now, for some reason that I never knew, I was called Sarah. I had become a triplet and had even changed nationalities: I had been born in New Zealand on 16 November 1970. I even had a passport to prove this. It may seem bizarre today but at the time I took this in my stride. I didn't even consider it strange that Anne had never given me this information before, or that previously I had been led to believe that I was someone else.

This sort of thing – sudden changes in our reality – was par for the course in our lives and we never questioned surprises. We were used to unpredictability as far as Anne was concerned. I hated the name Andrée anyway and being a triplet was more interesting than being a single sibling. I now know that there were several passports in my name, a couple of which were Australian. They all recorded different birth dates. I also had several birth certificates in different names and registered in different States.

I arrived in England in September or October 1984 and my going-through was to take place about a month later. My memories of that period are scant because it was one of the most traumatic times in my life, and a time of great change. But I will describe what I remember, as best I can, even though recalling that awful period always upsets me.

When I arrived at Broom Farm I was still consumed with guilt about the 'houses incident' and spent most of my time creeping around trying to be inconspicuous. By pretending to be invisible I thought I would actually be invisible. I felt so low that I wished I didn't exist. Mostly I was trying to stay out of Anne's range. She was still disgusted with me and she vented her disgust by being particularly vicious, deriding me in front of other cult members, telling them of my role in the 'houses incident' and of anything else that sprang to mind that she knew would embarrass me. She delighted in telling people how ugly and fat I was. I lurked around feeling horrible and embarrassed whenever I ran into anyone. I tried to pretend that what Anne said didn't hurt but in the end I felt I was little more than an eyesore.

I had always believed that it was my role to keep the peace at Uptop and I had let her down with my evil and base nature. In the time since the 'houses incident' I had tried very hard to be pure and spiritual, and even to control my thoughts, which despite myself continued to be cynical, sacrilegious and doubting. Anne's disdain just made me feel completely worthless.

As the day of my go-through approached there was a big build up, as there was for all the go-throughs. As it was such a great honour and also a religious ritual following on from the initiation ceremony, I felt like a sacrificial animal in the preceding days. People treated me differently, more gently. Although I felt considerable trepidation, having already seen something of what happened to initiates, I basked in finally being given some attention and noticed as a human being, in feeling that after this ordeal I might finally be considered an adult and treated as such.

It may seem strange that I could look forward to this 'sacred' rite. A short while beforehand I had watched one of my brothers, during his going-through, get down on his knees and beg me not to hate him for being a closet homosexual. This confession had been wrung out of him by Anne after several days of intensive 'working' under LSD. He felt that he was a failure, though I did my best to tell him that he'd never be a failure to me because I loved him. We were all scared of revealing our weaknesses but doubted that we would be able to hold anything back once under the influence of the drugs.

Finally the day of the 'go-through' arrived. I'd been up all the previous night wondering what was in store for me. In fact, we were forcibly deprived of sleep for several nights; we were meant to spend the time reading and further grasping the responsibilities of initiates to their guru outlined in *Yoga and the Bible*. I had been trying to concentrate on this, but all I could think about was how pathetic I was and how I would fail in this experience as I had failed in everything else. Early that morning I went for a walk around the fields with Scotty, our pet husky, hoping the adults would forget all about me and wishing that I could keep walking in the clear bright morning air for ever and not have to face the coming ordeal.

But at 9 or 10 o'clock that morning they sent Michael out to get me. I was allowed a piece of toast and then Anne ran the bath and I was told to get in. I couldn't believe it, Anne was actually looking after me. The guest bedroom was prepared. If I hadn't been so freaked out, I suppose I would have lapped up all the unaccustomed care and attention from Anne. After the bath I put on a short nightie and was told to get straight into bed. I didn't want to go to bed at that hour of the morning, I would have much preferred to spend more time walking in the fields with Scotty. But as usual what I wanted to do wasn't an option.

Anne came into the guest bedroom and gave me a piece of paper with a mandala printed on it and a little white tablet, which she said would help me hallucinate better. I had to chew the paper and I now know that it contained a dose of LSD, but I still do not know what the tablet was. Anne mentioned a name that sounded something like 'nitric acid'.

About half an hour after I had chewed the paper and swallowed the tablet I started to feel the effects. At first the light looked brighter, then everything looked clear cut, as if each object was delineated in its own aura of existence. It seemed as if everything was breathing, as if everything was alive. It was all utterly beautiful and yet completely terrifying.

Anne left me alone as soon as the drug began to take hold. She waited just long enough to satisfy herself that it was working. She turned out the lights so all I could see was a small glimmer through the curtains. That was the last light I saw for a very long time. I was all alone with the strange patterns in my head: weird shapes that hurtled at me out of the darkness, shapes like the little witches I used to imagine at night, which had scared me so when I was a child. I started to hyperventilate. Fear was building inside me. I wanted to escape.

All the time I struggled to maintain control of myself. I thought that if I gave in I would stop being me. I suppose I was also trying to challenge Anne's power: I was determined I would not make a fool of myself like others I had heard and seen, screaming and crying and acting like mad people under the drug. I still believed I could have some control over the process so I fought it. Yet at the same time I wanted it all to be over.

In fact, unconsciousness would have been a great blessing at times during that trip. It is hard to describe this without sounding melodramatic, but for a 14-year-old, an LSD trip is terrifying and the fact that it was forced on me made it more so. I was very scared and very vulnerable during that first go-through.

Even as I write about it now, I can almost taste the fear that I was experiencing. It felt as if my mind was slipping around inside my head. It felt as if each part of my body was separated from the other parts. It felt as if the skin and bone didn't link me to myself. I remember once looking at my hands in the dimness; they were shining, and then the skin seemed to writhe and crawl off them as if it had become maggots feeding on a corpse. The walls and ceiling of the dark room in which I was enclosed would recede into the distance, and then move in so close they could crush me. It seemed as if I and the bed in which I lay were alone in the universe.

And while all this was going on I was meant to be 'working'. This was a word used by Anne to mean using the drug to allow you to step back from the normal envelope of the self and have a good look at the inner parcel. At this point horrible things about yourself were supposed to be revealed to you, and then you could recant them, repent and be forgiven.

You were supposed to look at yourself and see the badness inside; to regress to significant incidents in childhood and in previous lives that had affected your personality and retarded your spiritual development. The drug, which Anne sometimes called the 'herb' or the 'dream medicine', was meant to make this easier. It was also meant to make the spiritual bonding easier between the Master and the disciple. You were supposed to recognise Anne as the 'one true Master', Christ incarnate. She would come in to people when they were under and ask, 'Do you know who I am?'. The correct answer was 'The Lord Incarnate'. The incorrect answer meant you weren't working hard enough.

Anne's technique of keeping us awake for several days before a go-through meant that we were incredibly vulnerable anyway. You have to hand it to Anne, she knew her stuff: this was chronic sleep deprivation and it increased the strain of the whole experience. Add to that the sensory deprivation, for I was placed in a quiet and dark room and never knew whether it was day or night. Even today, I find if I am really tired I'm prone to flashbacks from the LSD and it is harder to cope than it should be.

During the first day of my first go-through I was too scared to work effectively; I felt if I started concentrating on that process I would lose control and give in to the drug's power. Anyway, I didn't need a drug to help me find out how rotten I was. I already knew that only too well, after fourteen years of indoctrination. I was left alone all that day. I knew the day was passing from the noises coming up from the kitchen beneath, the sounds of the tables being set. Then came the silence of the night.

The drug was wearing off and I was very thirsty and hungry and tired. I wanted to sleep but I thought I should fight sleep. I was desperate to maintain control. Very late that night or it might have been early the next morning, Anne came in and gave me some more LSD. She chastised me severely for not working well enough. She said I needed an increased dose so that she could get me working properly.

After that I had no real idea of what was happening. Sometimes I would remember who I was and that I was going-through. Most of the time I was just floating. It seemed to go on for an age. Anne came in once or twice, and also sent messengers in to say that I should prepare for a spiritual experience and that I should repent of my selfishness and my sluttish desire to be raped whenever I was out on the street. At this stage of my life I didn't even know what rape was.

Eventually Anne came in once more, and made me curl into a ball, so that I could regress to babyhood. Nothing happened, probably because I didn't know what I was meant to do. But I managed to remember and re-experience a few bad things like the 'ants incident', and Anne took that as a sign that I was getting somewhere. She gave me some more LSD and told me to keep working and that I would get some good insights into myself before long.

I think that a few days and nights passed while I was in that state. I could only tell if another day had passed by the rattle of dishes in the kitchen below me as members prepared dinner each evening. I was completely terrified for almost the whole time and I still don't know how long I was kept drugged in that room. The drugs made it difficult to tell what was real and what was hallucination.

I am not sure what happened after that. I remember the door opened and a doctor came into the room, one of the doctors belonging to the cult. He sat on the bed. He said I was evil and that he had been sent by my Master to cure me. My evil, he said, was that subconsciously I was wanting to be raped. I didn't know what he meant by this.

I remember a feeling of terror spreading through me. He told me he was going to give me an operation 'to mix up your insides so you will never be able to have children', and that I would never want to think about sex again because I would be sick if I did. He said my guru had ordered this as a punishment for my filthy mind and as a lesson to teach me that God is more important than sex.

He had a knife. I think he cut me. I remember screaming. I thought that I felt the knife deep inside me. In the redness of the pain I heard Anne's laughter. She was in the room watching, goading him on. I thought that I heard her yelling, 'Perhaps that will teach you, you whore, you slut. We will give you what you want.' I felt the stickiness of the blood, my blood. I passed out.

That is all I consciously remember about my go-through. The rest is the stuff of nightmares. For years I used to relive the dreadful experience every September; the rest of the time I tried to forget it. It is only recently that I have gained any control over the nightmares; however, whenever I think about that go-through, I get a low aching in my stomach. I think I was abused, but how much is real and how much is drug-induced hallucination, I do not know. However, I have a scar that I don't remember existing before my going-through and I certainly did not receive it afterwards.

Regardless of whatever happened or did not happen, it changed my life. I left the 14-year-old Andrée behind forever. It was as if I had to sacrifice part of myself to survive the experience. After the go-through my concept of self changed and I existed in a daze of despair. It was like living in a black haze and functioning as some kind of a robot. I was able to speak and observe the social niceties, yet not know that I was doing so. I was not aware that I even existed. I think my mind was unable to cope with what I'd been through and it just left me there. My ability to analyse and to feel emotions was lost.

I sought refuge from Hell in Hell. Not that I consciously tried to get to that state. It just happened. I've since learnt that it isn't something the conscious mind has any control over. I know this because there have been times since when things have got too much for me, and I have tried to get back to that state to hide away from everything, and I haven't been able to.

I'm not sure how I can adequately analyse just what this state was that I retreated into. Perhaps it was a form of psychic splitting, of dissociation from the extreme psychological pain and emotions that were too difficult to face mentally at that time and still preserve my sanity and sense of selfhood. It was a primitive defence against emotional pain, a mental representation of curling up in a ball to avoid attack.

One day, as I was stepping into the car to go to Tunbridge Wells with Bill, I realised for the first time in months exactly what I was doing: I was stepping into a car with Bill. My hibernation was over and my identity had returned. I asked Bill what day it was and I remember being surprised by his answer. Even the month was a shock; I think a couple of months had passed. He said, 'You've been away a long time. It's good to have you back', which shocked me too because I thought he had not noticed.

It's hard to explain how much the first go-through affected me, but I know I've never been the same since. Andrée was dead and Sarah had been painfully born. I now believed that life was never going to be good or exciting; I'd lost the shine that even a childhood such as ours gives things. I decided then that life was a series of struggles and disappointments and that fate (or karma as I called it then) showed no mercy to anyone. I decided also that I could live without love because I was a survivor. I was so tough I was almost brittle, but I liked myself better than I had done when I was Andrée. Sarah had better control of herself than Andrée ever had. She wasn't always wishing things would get better. She could survive in a world without love. Sarah controlled her emotions because she denied she had any. I never cried in the days after my first go-through. I believed if I cried I would die; to cry would be to acknowledge the pain in my heart, the absolute desolation I felt at the most primal level. I did a good job of convincing myself that I was insensitive. It is only in more recent times that I have learnt once again to have feelings. I am still recovering from that first go-through.

Once I had gone through I gave up Baba as my guru. I felt that

I had to: I could no longer endure the duality of having two gurus. At a subconscious level I suppose I was very angry and disappointed that he had died and I could no longer count on him to save me in a spiritual sense. Paradoxically, although the experience of the go-through was an awful one, it cemented my status as one of Anne's disciples. I started to believe in her as my Master: I suppose I was terrified not to. I believed I had to accept the consequences of my initiation and learn to be a disciple of the path that I had not chosen, but was now forced to accept. Baba was no longer around to give me the chance to follow another spiritual path. Anne was now my Master and as her disciple I had to accept the sadhana (the spiritual discipline that occurs between initiation and final realisation).

I went through another three times when I was in England during that trip but those go-throughs weren't as traumatic as the first one, partly because I'd roped off part of my psyche and partly because I doubt that even purely on a physical level anything could be as bad again. The subsequent go-throughs only lasted about two days and by comparison they didn't seem to have much significance.

I ended up having a least a dozen go-throughs. In 1986, when I was 16, I went through three or four times, and once again at Crowther House, before I went back to England. By then my head was pretty messed up, and any LSD would send me off into flashbacks of the first experience. Anne used to plant 'control words' in the victim. These were hypnotic suggestions she would repeat while you were under the influence of the drug; she only had to say certain words to me on these occasions and I would experience a flashback. I cannot remember what the words were: in any event they have no power over me now. I believe that those sort of things, rather like pointing the bone and hypnotic suggestion in general, only have as much power as the victim is prepared to allow them.

Sometimes I tried to protect myself with a meditation trick when I went through. If you hyperventilate and concentrate very hard, you can go into a trance-like state or even lose consciousness and so escape the pain of reality. I used this as an adaptation method for go-throughs and also, after I had left the cult, when I was finding it too hard to cope because of my fear. I'd been taught to believe that if you thought 'wrongly' (which meant questioning Anne or even having cynical thoughts about her), you would be killed. I was very frightened in those days.

I have been present at many go-throughs of other cult members. When we were little, Uncle Leon went through at Uptop. We didn't know what was happening to him then of course: he was just acting strangely, crying and talking lots of nonsense. It was only later, after I had witnessed so many instances, and after I had experienced it myself, that I realised what must have been happening.

In about 1982 I saw Anne put herself through. At least I think she did. She started acting very strangely. I remember Shaun, who was meant to be our cousin, was visiting at the time and he said rudely that he thought she'd drunk too much. But looking back, I'd say she was on acid. She told us she was in samadhi, a state of ecstasy achieved by the holy ones, those who have attained enlightenment. We all had to sit around her feet while she made predictions about our futures. She said I'd have five babies!

I saw many people go-through at Broom Farm. I also saw all the older kids go-through, some of them a few times. Many people would scream and lose control. I was often ordered to sit with them as they weren't supposed to be left alone during a go-through. I was supposed to help them work by asking them questions with double meanings that would make them look into themselves.

When I was in England in 1984 a woman was rumoured to have gone mad during a go-through and run out into the snow. She is said to have died but I don't know any more than that. I was told that someone once died at Broom Farm in about 1976 and I think it was during a go-through. She was an old woman and it was said that she had had a heart attack. I remember that because when I first went through Anne told me I was lying in the bed in which someone had died and that her ghost would haunt whoever slept in that room. It was a good incentive not to go to sleep and was also guaranteed to inspire more terror.

Two of my brothers, Luke and Timothy, went through a couple of times when I was in England in 1984 and again when I was there in 1986. Neither of them was coping at their boarding school in England. Apparently they were treated appallingly there – bastardised because they were Australians and so different from the other kids. They had a bad time during their go-through. The first time they were together upstairs in the attic bedroom and Anne taunted both boys. Timothy became very angry. Apparently he had been raped when he was at the school; at least this is what Anne said. He seemed to relive the experience and it was horrifying for me to watch. Anne suggested to Timothy that he had enjoyed being raped because he was secretly a homosexual. This was a favourite suggestion of Anne's and I've heard her make it to many others. I've seen grown men break down under the attack of her repeated accusations while they were under the drug. She was always good at mental cruelty during go-throughs. This time, however, Timothy did not break down because his anger was too great.

Psylocibin mushrooms used to grow wild in the fields of Kent and in November they were in full season. They were highly hallucinogenic. Anne would sometimes use them instead of acid, to create a 'softer' trip; they were more hallucinatory than LSD but not as mind-blowing. They allowed a more pleasant trip and the fear of losing control was not as great.

I used to get sent out into the fields to collect these magic mushrooms for Anne. When Andrea was over there with me in 1984, it was our job to collect mushrooms as part of the morning chores. I also remember Anne frequently accompanying me on these field walks, and I would help her to spot the mushrooms. They were brown, grew about 50 millimetres tall and had a small bluish knob on the top. The knob distinguished them from field mushrooms.

The diameter of their bell was about a centimetre. They were only small and you had to take ten to twenty of them to produce a good effect.

Anne would order us to dry the mushrooms on sheets of paper in the back room. They were weaker when they were dry, but it meant she could use them out of season. They had a revolting taste and were slimy when fresh. They used to make me retch when I swallowed them. You had to block your nose and chew quickly and eat some chocolate afterwards to take the taste away.

When I was feeling so depressed that I longed to escape from reality, I would help myself to the mushrooms when I was sent out to pick them. Anne knew I was doing this and it made her angry with me. She wasn't too pleased about people deciding to enjoy their own trips.

CHAPTER 12

'Go and die in the gutter'

I returned from England in early 1985, a different person. I felt alienated from the other kids: no longer a child, although still not an adult. I knew now I wanted to prove myself and to escape from Uptop, but not in a physical way necessarily. I felt different, partly because the go-through had separated me from the others in experience, and partly because I felt I knew Anne better than the rest. I felt somehow special or chosen.

I also had a newly found boldness in my dealings with Anne; I felt, perhaps foolishly, that she and I had an understanding, that now that I knew better how she worked I could reason with her. At least now she noticed me and appeared to listen to what I said. I had thrown in my lot with her, had thrown myself into believing in her, so I rejected instead the Aunties. I blamed them for the cruelties and injustices in the system under which we lived. Anne was a goddess, untouchable; she was now my Master and I could not, for fear of my life, in an emotional, spiritual, and, I believed, physical sense, challenge her powers.

I loved her, I really did, as much as a kid without any emotional maturity at all could love. Her approval and love and attention meant the world to me. In a way, although I feel ashamed to admit it, I still *do* love her. This feeling is mixed with anger and sadness, and with bewilderment at the hurt she caused, but still there remains in me a small need for her approval and love.

She was the centre of my world for so long. I longed for her love and affection for so long. Sometimes I find myself wishing that all this had never happened and that we all lived in a fairyland fantasy world where we had all forgiven each other and could be nice to each other, and where I could believe that she *did* love and care for us all. Sometimes I wish that all the bad things I remember were just mistakes of discipline in a basically loving upbringing. Sometimes to believe in and live a lie is easier than facing the truth. Certainly Anne would have us believe that our childhood environment was a loving one, and I think she herself believes this.

We kids were all changing in those later years, growing up, becoming more cynical, gaining exposure to the outside world, and beginning to resent our isolation and strangeness. Our life was in some ways easier than it had been before. Yet we were unhappier, or at least more discontented, than before. Maybe it was partly because we had gained a self-awareness and the capacity to question. Apart from occasional instances, most of the harsh discipline had stopped – we no longer got regular beltings or missed out on meals for trivial things, even though the majority of rules were still enforced with the threats of losing privileges or doing lines. But the routine continued without change, inexorably.

We often asked the Aunties for explanations of why we were living Uptop, for explanations of the strange and rigid lifestyle and the bizarre assumptions about the outside world. They could never give satisfactory answers. I think all the adults were bewildered that we children were growing up, and they didn't know quite how to deal with it. Anne's master plan, such as it was, did not provide the answers. It was not adequate to deal with the growing self-awareness and diversity of personalities in a group of rapidly maturing adolescents. The Aunties couldn't quite cope with the fact that we were turning from children, who could be handled simply, like animals, into people who reasoned and argued and acted intelligently. It was hard for them when we questioned Anne; they had learnt to accept everything unquestioningly and to be afraid of any self-doubts.

We children were at an advantage: we thought that Anne was just our mother. I, of course, was initiated and shared some of the Aunties' fears, but I could at least separate mother from guru and level criticism at Anne's earthly traits while still revering her alleged spiritual ones. For the Aunties it was too threatening to question Anne in any way. They had joined the cult of their own volition and were true believers; we had been press-ganged into service and it was inevitable that some of us at least would want to seek a separate path.

We nagged constantly for more exposure to the outside world. We had seen little snippets of it occasionally during our lives – the trips overseas and the Dandenong singing experiences – and these transitory moments had left us, not with the distaste that we were encouraged to feel, but with an insatiable curiosity and need to experience more.

I feared I would be Uptop forever, and also that when the time came to function in the outside world I wouldn't be able to do so. I was acutely conscious of how different we were, without even having known any normal kids. I knew, despite what they tried to tell us of the value of our upbringing, that we could not survive out there: we had not the first clue. My doubts were only reinforced when we eventually did get to interact with some others of our own age.

Some time in 1985 Anne finally decided that we were going to be allowed some limited access to the outside world. This took the form of a trip for the older girls each week down to Melbourne to learn ballroom dancing. I think she realised that if we were not allowed some freedom we would rebel completely. On Friday evenings we went to a place in Upper Ferntree Gully called Kenlaurel Dance School. Five of us began and a sixth started a bit later. Every Friday night we travelled down with Aunty Helen to Crowther House in Olinda, got driven to the dancing school in Upper Ferntree Gully by Aunty Joy, Winberra's caretaker and Anne's right-hand woman, stayed at Crowther overnight and came back to Uptop with Uncle Leon on the Saturday morning. This was a big privilege, the denial of which was often held over us as punishment.

Crowther had about a dozen bedrooms. For one of the few times in our lives, we either had individual bedrooms or only two of us shared a room. We had been there only a few times: the night before the annual Dandenong Festival; and once for a two-week holiday with Anne, in about 1984. It was great fun for us there. The house was big enough to explore, the grounds were generous and we had exposure to television, radio and the outside world. In addition, when Anne was staying, there was much more excitement and a better diet than at Uptop.

Anne's ideas about our education were similar to those of English families who, in earlier times, sent their daughters to finishing schools on the Continent — something she often mentioned as part of her plans for our future. In the meantime, Anne thought dancing class would teach us the skills and social graces of refined ladies. Little did she know that we would dance to pop music, learn swear words and absorb some of the teenage culture of our new friends. Not that we had many. We were considered weird, with our strange clothing, dyed blonde hair and painful shyness. But Anna and I were befriended by two girls, Helen and Cathy, who became our pen-pals and our teachers, mentors and guides to the outside world.

In a way, ballroom dancing was the beginning of the end of our allegiance to the cult. Letting us go dancing was Anne's biggest mistake, although I'm sure she never dreamed it would lead to our corruption by the temptations of the world and our realisation that things were not right with Uptop. Through outside contact we learnt the world did not function as we had been taught to believe, and that children had rights. Through correspondence with Helen and Cathy over a couple of years, we slowly learnt about modern culture from a teenager's perspective. And while finding out that the outside world was so different from ours, we also learnt that it was not as horrible as we had been taught to believe. We learnt, too, that our way of life was considered extremely bizarre by 'normal' people. In the beginning the Aunties censored our letters to Helen and Cathy, although later they seemed to trust us not to say anything wrong about Uptop. But, even though we tried not to say anything that would be considered inappropriate, in just talking about our day-to-day life we couldn't help letting some things slip, and our pen-friends made it clear that they thought our lives were weird.

Due partly to this correspondence, we developed a taste for pop music and nagged the Aunties into letting us occasionally watch things like *Countdown* on television. We pressed Anne on her next visit to allow us to discard our silly smocks, and talked her into buying us wind-cheaters and giving us some of Natasha's old clothing, so we at least looked half-way normal, if still a trifle daggy. We even pinned up the posters of rock stars that Helen and Cathy sent us.

However, these posters caused the last big belting that I received from Bill. I'd put up Elvis Presley and a Nik Kershaw poster that Helen had sent us. Things had seemed to be getting a bit easier and Anne had even decided we could listen to pop music during our meals on the weekends. One Sunday morning Trish put on religious music instead of our pop music and I complained. Next weekend Anne came Uptop and ripped the posters down. She said I was a pervert and that I had put the posters up for sexual reasons. I was to be punished for being a sinner.

I felt guilty, though I hadn't done anything wrong. Anne started hitting me around the head with her hand, yelling, swearing and calling me a slut. She pushed me towards the door and told me to get to my room and wait for a belting. I went downstairs and waited for her and Bill. I remember the feeling of trepidation. I thought I deserved a belting though I didn't know why. Anne and Bill came in. They told me to take down my pants. Anne had a stiletto-heeled shoe in her hand and she started hitting me on my bare backside with the shoe. After about twenty or thirty hits she got tired and Bill took over. He hit me with his hands. My head kept hitting the wall and I saw stars. I could feel myself losing consciousness. I remember looking at Anne, pleading with her in my mind, and miraculously hearing her telling him to stop, and after a few more punches he did stop. As I said earlier, this was the only time I can ever remember Anne intervening to halt the punishment process.

That beating was horrible. At the time I believed Bill was going to kill me; he was so terrifying when he was out of control. Finally Anne and Bill left me. I don't know if I was bleeding. I don't know what my dazed thoughts were. It felt like the end. After the beating, I just sort of crawled into myself, and hid away from facing reality. It hurt too much to feel this bad.

Late in 1985 Anne allowed me to get a job on condition that I work as a secretary for Jim Macfarlane, the prominent cult member and physiotherapist who had a practice in Boronia. Although I had disliked him since childhood, I had no choice in the matter, and the job did give me the opportunity to see more of the outside world.

Every Thursday I came down to Winberra or Crowther with Aunty Lillibet, the music and speech teacher who usually visited and taught us on Wednesdays, then I worked at Jim's practice on Fridays, joining the others for dancing that evening. I am not sure why Anne allowed me this opportunity. I was paid 50 dollars for the day's work but was only allowed access to a few dollars of this; the rest was to be saved to pay for a trip overseas for me in 1986 to visit my triplet brothers in England. The job continued until I left the cult, and indirectly led to my expulsion from it.

Anne was home most of 1985, when I was 15, and we spent a fair bit of time with her at Crowther. She probably had more contact with us that year than she ever had, and it was also that year that she initiated some of the other older girls into the cult, and put them through under LSD for the first time. I was able to tell them what to expect when it was their turn to go-through. I had one more short experience myself at Crowther, but by then I was knowledgeable about the effects of the drug. I was too experienced in watching the way Anne performed, having witnessed many go-throughs, to be sucked into working hard, confessing anything or getting too frightened. Not so the others. I helped when Andrea and Megan went through Uptop, and when Anna, Arrianne and Susanne went through at Crowther not long after.

'Helping' largely involved just sitting with the girl involved, prodding her and supporting her if she was having insights or confessions or experiencing bad things. Between times, Anne, or one of the senior Aunties (Christabel at Crowther and Trish and Wynn at Uptop) would come in and goad her, or try to elicit a confession, or just generally try to mindfuck the person in her confused state. For the sake of people's privacy, I will not reveal what went on: suffice to say that it was the usual stuff of trying to instil guilt and self-reproach about sexuality and relationships.

In those days of late 1985 we were becoming cheekier than ever. And even keener to get out of Uptop. I felt stifled by the limited schoolwork we were given. Essentially, once we passed primary school level our 'school' lacked the resources to teach us much more than maths.

It was up to each individual to learn as best he or she could from the textbooks that Leon Dawes brought from Croydon High School. Not surprisingly, with the onus being entirely on the individual to learn, our education was a hit and miss affair. At this point I realised that our education would never be recognised in the outside world – and that education would be my only passport out of Uptop. If I could get my Higher School Certificate (HSC) somehow, there would be a chance that I could go on to study at a college or university.

But Anne did not believe that girls should receive an education. Girls in the cult were supposed to be 'ladies', trained to knit and sew and taught manners, singing and speech. The only profession considered for us was nursing. Only boys were worthy enough to have money spent on sending them to school. My triplet brothers were sent to boarding schools in England when they were 14, while

I had to beg and plead to be allowed to learn.

I managed to convince Anne, with much wheedling and playing of the mind games in which she so loved to indulge, to allow me to start Year Eleven via correspondence. The adults had discovered how to manipulate the correspondence school system a couple of years before when they had enrolled Stephen, who was legally blind. You were only supposed to use correspondence school if you were geographically isolated or had such a severe physical or mental disability that you could not attend a regular school. But it was a simple thing for Anne, with cult doctors on tap, to apply on my behalf, supplying bogus medical information. I was duly enrolled, on the pretence of poor eyesight.

I loved the correspondence work. For the first time in years, I felt intellectually challenged. I picked up physics and social studies. The most we had ever done before in chemistry was learn a list of the elements. I discovered English literature and critical writing and expanded my previously limited experience of English expression.

At Uptop we had learnt a smattering of Latin, we had been given formal grammar, we had been taught basic anatomy and physiology by one of the doctors of the cult, our maths skills were far above average, and we could all spell well, and read and write articulately. But I cannot agree with cult members when they say we had a superior education, a claim that they have made and continue to make as a justification for the entire nature of our upbringing.

In a lot of things we were sadly lacking. It is true that a couple of us managed to get our HSC and go on to higher education, but the majority struggled at school after they left the cult. The luckiest were the youngest because in the lower grades of school they had the time and opportunity to make up for the deficiencies in our education. But those who tried to go into Year Eleven or Twelve in outside schools, after we left the cult, had not only to battle with fitting in and meeting the rigid social expectations of a senior school, but also to adapt to a whole new educational system. Most did not last.

I often meet people who, on learning how well I did at university, say to me that I should thank the cult for my good education. This implies that things can't have been all that bad at Uptop. I get incredibly annoyed at the blind assumptions made by these people; at the inference that they know better than I do how to interpret the significance or validity of what happened in my childhood. They don't know anything about it at all, only the somewhat distorted picture exposed by the media. All I can thank the cult for is teaching me to read, write and spell, and for instilling in me the value of self-discipline (albeit by brute force). But my secondary education was largely self-taught and the most I can thank Anne for was allowing me to attend the correspondence school, at which I could learn at my own pace without having to face surviving in an outside school.

Anne went back to England in early 1986. We continued going to dancing class. I continued working for Jim Macfarlane, I kept writing to my pen-pals, Cathy and Helen, and I began doing Year Eleven at correspondence school. My teachers there were good, although slightly eccentric. They saw promise in my early bumbling attempts and they nurtured me. I did well at Year Eleven. In November I went with Aunty Joy to England and spent Christmas at Broom Farm with Luke and Timothy. As Anne was there, we celebrated Christmas. My relationship with Anne intensified and we finally started conversing on a semi-adult basis.

It helped too that I was growing better looking; I was no longer the awkward, unattractive, painfully shy teenager I had been in England two years before. I was more sure of myself at 16 (or when I thought I was 16), or at least more sure of the way the cult worked and how to get on with Anne. Or so I thought. But still, in retrospect, I was miserably depressed even though I now received far more attention and affection from Anne.

That trip to England in late 1986 was an interesting one for me. Luke and Timothy had changed quite a lot. When they left Uptop in early 1984, they had been pre-pubertal, very short, and rather strange with their blond hair and Uptop shyness, mannerisms and figures of speech. We had all been chronically shy children; we had trouble looking people in the face and were deeply embarrassed by personal attention. Now, after two years away, the boys were unrecognisable.

They had grown about 30 centimetres, changed their hair, and begun to sport British public school accents, deep voices and an air of desperate bravado. The bashings that they had had to endure at school, on account of their difference, had taught them to adapt, but at great psychological cost. Anne had not made things easier for them by capitalising on their vulnerability and tormenting them under numerous LSD trips.

With Luke and Timothy home at Broom Farm on Christmas school holidays, we had a good time, although I remember Luke was already quite depressed. This was largely because he was being treated very badly by Anne. Timothy, now the better looking of the boys, had become the golden boy and Luke was reviled.

At first Luke still tried to impress Anne, working like a slave around the farm, quietly going about doing hard and dirty jobs. When she failed to notice, he withdrew into himself. During one of Luke's go-throughs Anne had said he would become an alcoholic and die. Almost inevitably he took to alcohol, desperate for her to notice him and love him. I felt very sorry for him that his life was made so miserable by a trick of nature.

It was during this visit that I first discovered alcohol and first got drunk with my triplet brothers. There was a pub just a few hundred metres up the road from Broom Farm, and we would seek permission to take the dogs for a walk, and then go for a drinking session instead.

The boys also smoked, and Timothy secretly had a motorbike at school, hidden from Anne and Bill. Neither of the boys was doing well in school, and they had changed schools a few times. In the end neither finished, although Luke, at least, was more than clever enough to pass.

While I was in England, Anne insisted that I get a job as she did not want to give out pocket money, so I found work as a dishwasher and kitchen-hand in a café run by friends of hers. Having never been in a kitchen before, I was pretty hopeless at preparing food: I remember I did not even know how to grate cheese when they asked me to do so. These friends of Anne's also owned the chemist shop next door and after a couple of days promoted me to working as a perfumery assistant. That was how I ended up serving rich Arabs in downtown Tunbridge Wells, while still remaining almost totally ignorant of the outside world and still within the cult.

Anna, left behind in Australia, ran away while I was overseas. She had tried to run away once before, many years earlier when she was about 12 or thirteen. She had gone around the lake's edge and finally knocked on the door of one of the houses close to the waterfront. The people there had rung the Eildon police who took Anna to the station and rang Uptop. Far from believing her story, they allowed themselves to be bluffed by the Aunties. Trish and Helen went into Eildon to pick her up. They told the police that she was a disturbed child, that she made up stories and had trouble controlling her emotions. They reassured the police that she was being medicated by a doctor for her problems. Indeed, Anna was viewed as sick after that and given extra sedation. As in Stalinist Russia, if you questioned the system, you got labelled as ill. I will never forgive those policemen for not listening to my sister at that time. I know the story probably sounded far-fetched to them, but sometimes children's stories are not just the stuff of imagination. I think the police did visit Uptop not long after that and question us, but again they were fobbed off by the lies of the Aunties and our well-rehearsed answers to their questions.

Anyway, this time Anna ran away and didn't come back. It was a tremendous scandal, and I think it shook cult members a lot. Anna was formally disowned by Anne and Bill: no one was allowed to utter her name or talk about her; she was no longer part of our Family. She was designated a traitor. Anne said she was now a whore on the streets and stole and sold drugs to make money. This smear campaign was nothing unusual: everyone who ever left The Family was subjected to it. But this was the first time one of the children had run away. Unfortunately, most of us believed at least part of what Anne was saying, having so little knowledge of what Anna could actually do or how life worked in the outside world. Not one of us really understood what it meant to be a prostitute and a druggie, though we guessed these were vulgar things to be.

This time I refused to comply with the cult in erasing the memory of someone who had defected. It was the usual stuff: someone did the cult wrong and everyone pretended the person had never existed. No mention of the traitor was allowed and all physical evidence was removed. I refused to deny that one of my sisters even existed and this meant I was going against the system or, more specifically, going against Anne.

When I came back to Australia in early 1987 I went to live at Winberra, although I went Uptop with Leon Dawes at weekends. I had convinced Anne to agree to this. At Winberra it would be easier for me to receive the correspondence school mail and to attend seminars and practical work at the school's headquarters in the city. I was enrolled to start HSC. I was to continue with the correspondence course for the rest of my secondary education, during the biggest social and emotional upheaval I would ever know.

I had told Anne that, once I was living at Winberra, out of the way of corrupting the rest of the kids, I would do everything I could to find Anna, for I still considered her my sister. I tried to convince Anne that she should not indulge in histrionics, but rather be merciful and treat Anna as would any other understanding parent of a teenage runaway, and support her if she came back. But Anne was immovable. She believed that she had received a personal insult, and Anna was not going to be forgiven for betraying The Family.

My new living arrangements only worked for a few weeks

before things began to go wrong. Anne, still in England, inexplicably started to make my life miserable. Even though she was overseas she was in constant contact with the Aunties. She made repressive rules that applied only to me and she was suspicious about everything I did. This hostility may have been a knee-jerk reaction to my stated intention of finding Anna, because, true to my word, I started looking for her. Before Anna left she had been doing a course by correspondence, so I rang her Technical and Further Education college. They had an old address. On the pretence that I was going to a correspondence school seminar, I fearfully (for I was very scared of public transport and of being on my own) ventured down to Gold Street in Collingwood and left a note at the house that, unbeknown to me, Anna had long since left, saying that I wanted to catch up. A couple of months later I got a letter in reply, and joyously we met again.

Meanwhile Anne was making my life hell at Winberra. She forbade me to go Uptop, saying my attitude was bad. She accused me of going out and whoring, and made me draw up an outline of my daily routine, ordering that it be signed and counter-signed by Joy and Vera, the two Aunties who lived at Winberra. These two had started to spy on me, particularly when I was talking on the phone to Anna. Soon that privilege was stopped, as was the privilege of using light or electricity in the house, on the pretext that I was being wasteful. I was forced to go across the road to another cult member's house to study because it was so dark at Winberra, and also to use the shower because the bottom part of the house was locked to me on the pretext that I had 'bad vibrations'.

I was spending as much as eighteen hours a day studying, determined to do well and win back the favour I had lost. I tried desperately to talk to Anne. I wanted to sort out what was going on: I didn't understand why she had turned against me. I wanted her to explain herself to me. This was, in her view, an unforgivable arrogance in itself, and worthy of more punishment. Certainly I was being rebellious, but I loved her and believed in her still, and did not understand why I was being punished so severely.

The worst of it was Anne's silence and contempt. She refused to talk to me: she only sent snide and cryptic messages through other cult members. I was puzzled because I had thought I had reached a better understanding with her, and that we could have talked through any problems. I still naively assumed she was a rational being, and also that she would listen to and understand my side of the story. Things reached a stalemate. I was desperately miserable at Winberra, and unsure of how I could get back in favour – or indeed, in the end, whether I wanted to. For the first time in my life I was angry at the unfairness of it all, and determined to stick up for myself.

Then one Friday afternoon, when I was working for Jim Macfarlane – I'd gone back to my old job there – who should walk into the clinic but Helen and Cathy, our old pen-pals from the dancing school, with their mother, Erica. They immediately invited me to have tea with them in a day or so and I gratefully accepted. According to the rules at Winberra, I was allowed to go out one night a week until 8 o'clock. The last bus went past at 6, and there was no other way of getting back, so I had not taken advantage of being allowed out before, except once to visit Anna.

At dinner with Erica and her family, I started, for the first time in my life, to talk a little about how miserable I was and what was going on in my life. Erica wrote me a letter after that evening telling me, among other things, that eventually I had to be my own person. In part that letter gave me the courage for what followed.

When Erica drove me back up the mountain because I'd missed the bus, I invited her into the house. I knew in the outside world it was a polite thing to do, to invite someone in for a cup of tea if they had given you a lift home. But in our world it was a heinous crime. The cult motto 'Unseen, Unheard, Unknown' was pounding through my head as I let Erica inside. No stranger was ever allowed into Anne's house. Apart from social niceties, even to talk to a stranger was forbidden, and to give them information about how we lived was one of the worst sins possible. It was considered treason and betrayal. I knew this: I was deliberately baiting Anne, hoping to force a confrontation. I knew Anne would finally have to talk to me, if only to scream abuse and administer a new punishment. I was dreadfully scared, but also determined to end the stupid and senseless stalemate.

Sure enough, I was called in early the next morning to speak to Anne on the phone as the Aunties had reported me during the night. There was screaming and ranting that I had gone too far, and threats that if I did not watch my step I would be disowned as Anna had been. That day a telegram arrived for me from England: 'Do not bring strangers into my house ever again. Father'. I brazened it out. I wanted an outcome. The very next week I returned to Erica's for dinner, and then repeated my crime.

The Aunties could do nothing about it: they had to be polite to Erica while she was there and pretend to be nice to me, but I was really in trouble. This time, retribution was swift. Anne telephoned and coldly gave me an ultimatum.

'You will get out of my house', she said. 'Go and live at Aunty Liz's.' (This was the dank, dismal house across the road where I had been studying.)

At that point I could have retracted and saved myself, and the course of my life may have been different. I could have recanted, and repented of my crime, endured her rage and tried to worm my way back into favour. After all, she was finally talking to me. But something within me snapped: I finally and for the first and last time refused to crawl.

'I will not live in Elizabeth's house, and I want you to stop treating me like a piece of shit', I replied. 'I am in no way sorry for what I have done, and would do it again tonight. I don't care about your stupid, petty rules.'

I said this rather shakily because I knew I was virtually signing my death warrant if she was not willing to be merciful. She was not.

'Right, you have twenty-four hours to get out of my house. You are no longer our daughter. Go out there – go and die in the gutter.'

With those words I was thrown out of the cult, and my world changed forever. I packed up my schoolwork and my few clothes and walked out into the world beyond. I had no idea what to do, or how to survive, and Anne knew that. I think she expected me to spend a few days curled up in the gutter somewhere and starving, and then creep back, humbled and repentant. Alternatively, I might have died. Either of these options was probable for now that I had lost favour with my Master, I had little will to survive. Still, sometimes we get strength from unexpected places.

I walked up to the top of the road and sat down. Where to from here? And then I remembered that Erica had given me her telephone number and told me to ring her if I ever got into trouble. She and her family were the only people I knew in the outside world. I went to the public phone at the milk bar opposite where I sat, and dialled the number. Erica answered. I told her that I had been kicked out.

Erica said to me simply, 'Wait five minutes and I will come and pick you up. You are welcome to stay with us as long as it takes for you to find your bearings.'

CHAPTER 13

The raid

I stayed with Erica and her three children in Upper Ferntree Gully from May 1987 through the early months of winter until August. It was due to Erica's kindness that I survived my introduction to the outside world. I don't remember a great deal of those few months. I loved my schoolwork; sometimes it was my only life-line to sanity, the only stable thing in that time of great upheaval, change and revelation. I studied obsessively day and night, grateful for this one constant in my life, and forever I will thank my lucky stars that I was enrolled in correspondence school because it was the only way I could have acquired an education in the circumstances in which I found myself. Studying was the only thing in life at which I could succeed and all that insane year I continued despite everything. I ended up dux of the school in 1987, the largest school in Australia although I didn't know any of the other students!

At Erica's I learnt things about normal families, things that filled me with wonder and also an acute sense of loss, without really knowing just what it was that I had lost. I saw how Erica and her children interacted, the concern they felt for each other without ever considering it, the love they took as their innate right, with no thought of having to earn it or of having to prove themselves worthy of that love. This was a novel concept to me: the thought of children being given unconditional love, of being inherently precious.

And it was through Erica that I came to meet Helen D., a private investigator who had been following The Family for several years. Helen began to tell me all about who I was, and who Anne was, and the real nature of The Family. It was what I discovered from Helen that made me fall apart.

My grip on reality at that time was already tenuous. The strain on my psyche from all the changes and adaptations that I had to make was enormous. I had to learn many things to survive in this new world, and the challenges to all the beliefs that I had held and cherished as a *raison d'être* for existence were too much.

I fainted when Helen first told me on the phone that I was not a Hamilton-Byrne and never had been, and that the woman I had held up on a pedestal for so long as mother and spiritual teacher was nothing but a fraud, only out to get people's money and their souls.

I would not believe it at first; I could not. My system could not cope with this overload: I retreated into a catatonic state. This was the only defence mechanism I had to deal with overwhelming pain and emotions, a defence mechanism I had learnt as a child to escape from an inescapable situation, and which I had perfected while going-through. I think I spent several days like that, but somewhere deep inside me I understood that what Helen was saying was true, and that I could not run from it forever.

If it had not been for Erica's demonstrable kindness and love, and the vast differences that I witnessed every day between the light and laughter of her household and the darkness of Uptop, I don't think that I would have ever accepted the truth. I was constantly faced with the glaring discrepancy between the fantasy of 'love' that we had experienced and the facts of ordinary, everyday, outside-world love. Without Erica and her family it would have been too easy to take shelter in delusion – to assume, as we had been taught to do, that I was being tempted to be unfaithful, and close myself off totally from any alternative explanation of the facts. But the demonstrable hypocrisy of our past finally saved me.

Eventually, I gathered myself together a little and wanted to find out more. Who was I if I was not a Hamilton-Byrne? I went to the Registry of Births, Deaths and Marriages. I remember my feeling of despair when I found out that there was no such person as Sarah Dominique Hamilton-Byrne in the State of Victoria. Officially I did not exist: my identity and, by extension, the rest of my world and cherished beliefs were a lie.

Helen advised me to apply under the name Hubble because that was the name under which I had been adopted into the cult. She'd learnt this information from her many years of investigation into The Family. Sure enough there was a record for an Ondre Lenore Hubble, but she – I – had been born on a completely different date from that which I had been told was my birthday. I had been born on 8 July 1969: I was nearly two years older than I had thought. I'd aged almost two years in a day!

With the help of Helen, I found the papers that handed me over from Beryl Hubble (a general practitioner and cult member) to Anne, the papers that then changed my name from Hubble to Hamilton-Byrne, and the papers that finally made Anne my legal guardian. And curiously, there were papers that changed Beryl Hubble's name several times: to Christine Fleming and then Anne Hamilton-Byrne. So it became evident that I had been adopted, and my name changed first to Ondre Lenore Hamilton Hubble.

In 1974 Beryl Hubble appointed Anne Hamilton-Byrne as guardian of Andrée Lenore Hamilton Hubble. At the same time Anne Hamilton-Byrne informally dropped Hamilton as my third Christian name and Hubble as my surname and gave me the new surname of Hamilton-Byrne. Then, to confuse matters further, on 11 July 1975, Beryl Hubble changed her own name by deed poll to Anne Hamilton-Byrne and, representing herself as the mother of Andrée Lenore Hubble, legally changed my name to Andrée Lenore Hamilton-Byrne. I had an Australian passport (Number 25803) in this name. Much later, in 1984, Anne, as my legal guardian, changed my name to Sarah Dominique Hamilton-Byrne and acquired a New Zealand birth certificate and passport (Number A605987) for me.

I was now certain that I had been adopted. I applied to find out the names of my real parents. I was sent a letter saying that there was a six-year waiting list. I still had no clue who I was. I had acquired a baptismal certificate and numerous birth certificates for Sarah Hamilton-Byrne and for Andrée Marguerite Hamilton-Byrne from New Zealand, Western Australia and New South Wales – all giving different ages and showing me to be the daughter of Anne and Bill. I felt betrayed as I looked at Anne's familiar signature on those pieces of paper. There in black and white was irrefutable evidence that everything I had believed to be true and had taken for granted was a lie. My whole life was a lie.

This information took an enormous psychological toll on me. I found it hard to cope in those early days. Erica was very generous and kind, but it was hard for her children having a 'weirdo' living in their house. I had many days when I was normal and enjoyed being with the family, learning things like how to ride a push-bike, finding out about teenage values and mores, and enjoying the liveliness and cheekiness of discussion and banter that was characteristic of their family life. But I had other days when I was very fragile, consumed by terror that what I was learning and coming to believe constituted a betrayal of my initiation vows and so would earn me the penalty for treason to the Master: death, spiritual as well as physical.

I started to confide in Erica and, later, a little in Helen, although I was less sure that I could trust her. But there was bursting within me a need to confide in someone, for someone to know my background and so gain some understanding of how it had made me who I was now. That is still an occasional intense need within me today: a need to articulate experiences of the past and be understood because of them and accepted despite them.

One weekend I went back to Uptop with Helen D. We stayed in the Eildon caravan park, and under cover of night I sneaked into the property I knew so well, climbed into the house via the toilet window, and went into the downstairs girls' bedroom to talk with Annette and Julieanne. I went because I wanted to see how

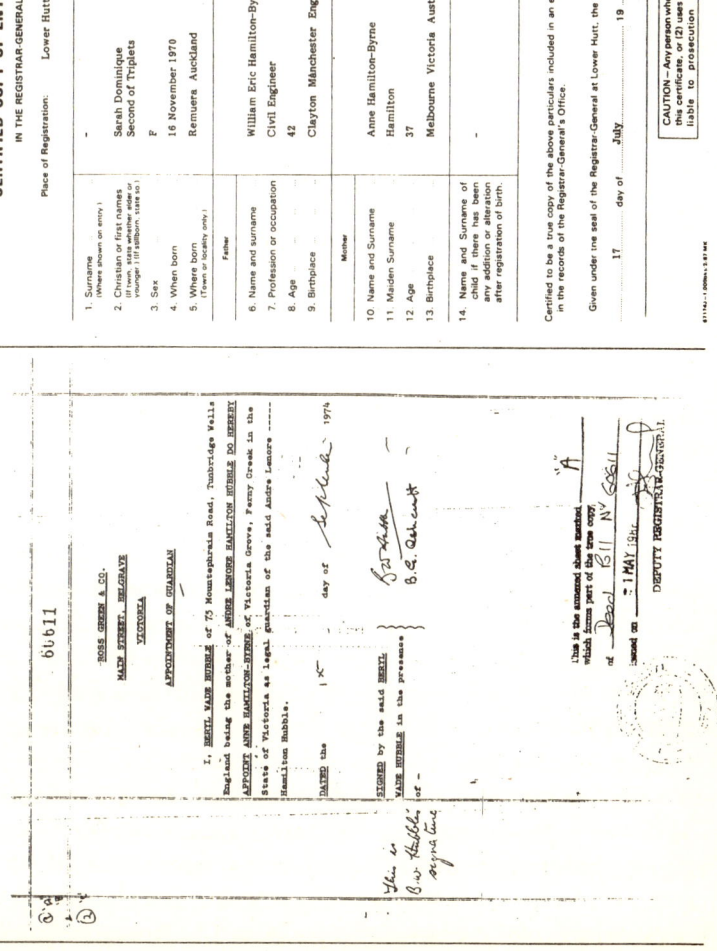

TWO OF MY MANY OFFICIAL DOCUMENTS

R.G. 100

NEW ZEALAND
CERTIFIED COPY OF ENTRY OF BIRTH   Nº 34999

IN THE REGISTRAR-GENERAL'S OFFICE

Place of Registration: Lower Hutt

1. Surname (Where shown on entry): —
2. Christian or first names (If twin, state whether elder or younger) (If stillborn, state so): Sarah Dominique / Second of Triplets
3. Sex: F
4. When born: 16 November 1970
5. Where born (Town or locality only): Remuera Auckland

Father

6. Name and surname: William Eric Hamilton-Byrne
7. Profession or occupation: Civil Engineer
8. Age: 42
9. Birthplace: Clayton Manchester England

Mother

10. Name and Surname: Anne Hamilton-Byrne
11. Maiden Surname: Hamilton
12. Age: 37
13. Birthplace: Melbourne Victoria Australia
14. Name and Surname of child if there has been any addition or alteration after registration of birth: —

Certified to be a true copy of the above particulars included in an entry of birth in the records of the Registrar-General's Office.

Given under the seal of the Registrar-General at Lower Hutt, the 17 day of July 19 87.

CAUTION — Any person who (1) falsifies any of the particulars on this certificate, or (2) uses it as true, knowing it to be false, is liable to prosecution under the Crimes Act 1961.

6u611

ROSS GREEN & CO.
MAIN STREET, BELGRAVE
VICTORIA

APPOINTMENT OF GUARDIAN

I, BERYL WADE HUBBLE of 73 Mountephraim Road, Tunbridge Wells England being the mother of ANDRE LENORE HAMILTON HUBBLE DO HEREBY APPOINT ANNE HAMILTON-BYRNE of Victoria Grove, Ferny Creek in the State of Victoria as legal guardian of the said Andre Lenore Hamilton Hubble.

DATED the 1st day of September 1974

SIGNED by the said BERYL WADE HUBBLE in the presence of —

B.S. Calcutt

This is the annexed sheet marked which forms part of the true copy of Decl Bill Nº 6611

Issued on 7 MAY 19...

DEPUTY REGISTRAR-GENERAL

they all were. I was worried that Cassandra might be starving to death. I was worried about Stephen, too; his fits were inadequately controlled and so was his behaviour. The regimen at Uptop was vastly inappropriate for an autistic child. I also felt guilty that my leaving may have got the children into trouble. And I wanted to remember what it was like Uptop in that other world I had called home for so long. I felt a tearing within me – I needed to convince myself finally that what was happening up there was wrong before I could agree with the interpretations of outsiders.

I found the house in turmoil. David had been locked in the upstairs bathroom without food for several days and had been given many severe beatings by Trish for cheekiness. Bill was due back from overseas within days, and the cult was extremely paranoid because Natasha – Anne's natural daughter – had defected. This was obviously a major defection. Anne's rationalisation of the situation was that Natasha had gone mad. (Natasha returned to the cult a few years later, for a brief period, before leaving The Family for good.)

The remaining kids were feeling very restless and rebellious. They did not believe all the lies they'd been told about Anna and myself: that we were whoring on the streets, using drugs and selling ourselves to the police. Luckily, though, Cassandra was still alive and her diet had even slightly improved.

I gave Annette and Julieanne postage stamps so they could post letters to me. I had made an arrangement with some Uptop neighbours that if the girls could sneak out of the property and leave letters on their doorstep, they would post them on to me. I told my sisters that there were people in the world who really cared about them. They didn't believe me. They couldn't conceive of anything like that, and they later wrote me letters confirming their disbelief, letters which I've still got. They asked me if I was a traitor like Natasha, but believed me when I reassured them that I wasn't. I was very moved by seeing them again. I wanted to see David, to check how he was, but the girls talked me out of it, deciding that it was too risky for me to go upstairs. Aunty Trish was still awake

Towards a new life, 1987. (Courtesy the *Australian*.)

David's first-ever ride on a bicycle, outside our unit at Allambie, a few days after the raid on Kai Lama in August 1987.

Doctor Christabel Wallace. She was convicted in 1990 of making a false declaration that she had witnessed the birth of triplets (me, Timothy and Luke) to Anne Hamilton-Byrne. (Courtesy the Melbourne *Age*.)

Four of the 'Aunties' who were convicted of falsely obtaining social security payments and given five-month gaol sentences (reduced on appeal) were photographed at the time.

Elizabeth Whitaker, aged 64, was convicted of falsely obtaining nearly 23 000 dollars between 1983 and 1987. (Courtesy the Melbourne *Age*.)

Margot MacLellan, aged 64, was convicted of falsely obtaining about 28 000 dollars between 1978 and 1988. (Courtesy the Melbourne *Age*.)

Joy Travellyn, aged 56, was convicted of falsely obtaining over 38 000 dollars between 1979 and 1988. (Courtesy the Melbourne *Age*.)

Helen Buchanan, aged 49, was convicted of falsely obtaining almost 15 000 dollars between 1980 and 1987. (Courtesy the Melbourne *Age*.)

My mother, in about 1972.

My mother and father's wedding day.

Elizabeth Whitaker leaves the court in September 1993. Like Anne and Bill, she was charged with conspiracy; however, the prosecution did not proceed. (Courtesy the Melbourne *Age*.)

In 1993 Anne and Bill were extradited from the United States to stand trial on charges of conspiring to commit perjury in relation to the false registration of the births of Timothy, Luke and me in New Zealand. Photographed leaving the Melbourne Magistrates' Court in August, Anne for once was caught without her wig and elegant clothes. (Courtesy the Melbourne *Age*.)

Anne looked extraordinarily youthful and glamorous arriving for a court hearing in November 1993 on Bill's arm. Roland Webb, the adopted son of Elizabeth Whitaker and Don Webb, is on the right. (Courtesy the Melbourne *Age*.)

Anne leaving the County Court in September 1994 after being fined 5000 dollars for making a false declaration that Timothy, Luke and I were her natural-born triplets. The Supreme Court had earlier ruled that the more serious charge of conspiracy could not be sustained in the State of Victoria since it concerned New Zealand. (Courtesy the Melbourne *Age*.)

I was subpoenaed to attend the County Court proceedings, but in the end was not required to give evidence because Anne and Bill pleaded guilty to the lesser charge of making a false declaration. (Courtesy the Melbourne *Age*.)

One of my small friends at the River Kwai hospital in December 1993 – much happier after recovering from malaria.

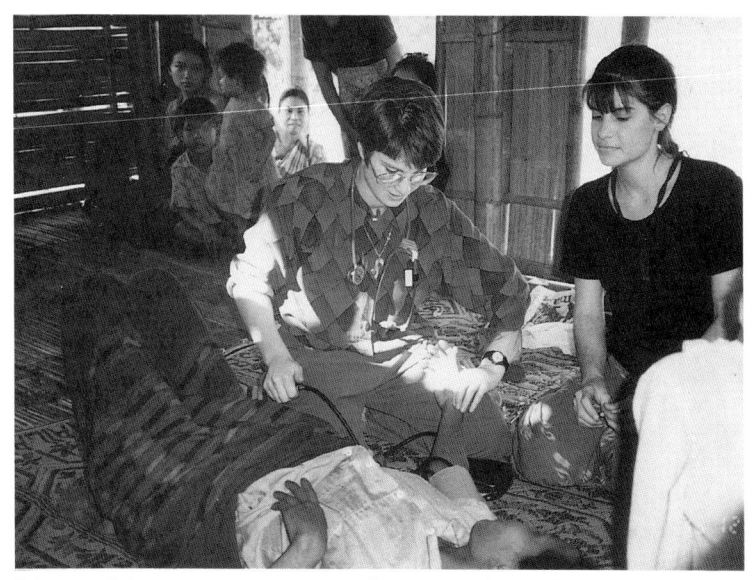

Me examining pregnant women at the Maternal Health Centre at Hti Hta Baw refugee camp. Many of the women were smaller than their dates indicated, and examination picked up several serious complications.

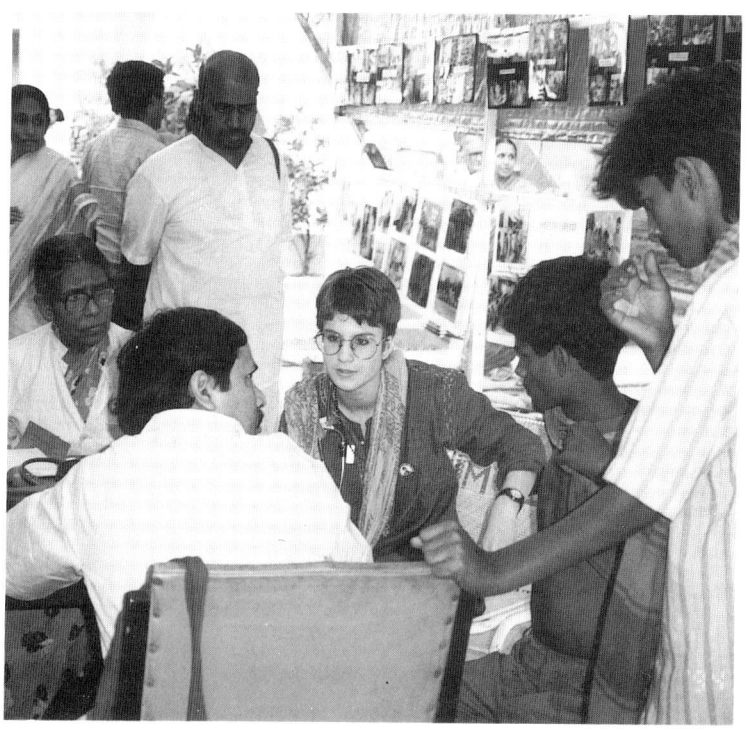

In Calcutta during November 1994 I worked with the mobile medical unit of the Ramakrishna Mission. Here I am discussing a patient's skin condition with another doctor.

My mother and me.

Graduation day, 10 December 1994.

and there was also a fear that if Benjamin woke he might dob me in to the Aunties or, at least, tell them that I had been. Before I left I tried to convince them that if they got kicked out they would not be alone.

Leaving the children that night, I felt very helpless. I felt terrible that David was locked in the bathroom and that I couldn't see him and reassure him that I cared about him. I felt more than ever that what was happening to the kids was wrong, that we should be allowed to talk to each other as brothers and sisters and that the discipline was unnecessarily cruel.

Back in Melbourne, Helen D. started pressing Anna and me to talk to the police. Anna was also a good friend of Erica and her family (through her earlier pen-friend relationship with Cathy), and I had seen quite a bit of her while I was living there. She, too, had met and spoken with Helen. Unlike me, Anna seemed to feel no compunction in denouncing Anne and the cult: there was not the same crisis of faith, although I am sure the process of surviving and adapting had been just as hard and she had had to find enormous courage to do it alone. Unlike me, she had not had the luxury of living with a loving and sympathetic family. She had ended up on the streets of Collingwood, moving from one group house to another, finding work and company as best she could, and totally relying on her wits to survive. I admired that: I never would have had the courage. Without Erica's support I would simply have 'died in the gutter' as Anne had commanded or, if not, probably crawled back to The Family, submissive and contrite.

We also saw a bit of Andrea, who was doing her HSC in a school in Melbourne, paid for by a trust left to her by her real grandparents. If that money had not been there she would never have gone to school, because Anne would not have paid for a girl's education. Andrea, too, met Helen, and decided that she would talk to the police. I was still distrustful and scared of police, as I think we all were, and was not willing to talk, although I felt an urgency to do something about the plight of the others, especially that of Stephen and Cassandra. Now that we had discovered that in the outside world there were people who would look after our well-being, it did not seem a grave sin to help the other children and to introduce them to such people. Still, I could not agree to talk to the police. I was too scared of the uniform and of the corruption and treachery that I had been led to expect would follow any communication with the law.

While I was living at Erica's some of the kids rang me. Annette, in particular, rang regularly and I asked her if she could get a copy of a tape that Anne had sent to the children, talking about me and denouncing and abusing me. I wanted her to bring it with her to the next Dandenong Festival. I also wanted them to send me a page from the rule books. They did that and got caught, and after that the phone was locked in the larder and they missed out on their food and were given the 'Judas treatment' (told they were treating Anne the same way Judas had treated Christ). Apparently when Julieanne was asked during an interrogation by Leon whether she would do it again, she said, 'Oh, it depends on the circumstances'.

In these ways I was gathering plenty of information about the cult, and yet I was still too scared to go to the police. Actually I thought if I did I would be killed. I knew that, however good my intentions, I would be cursed by Anne and my actions would be regarded as a betrayal, the penalty for which was death in a particularly horrible manner – with no hope of salvation.

We had seen and heard of Anne placing curses on people and believed they always came true. I have described earlier a few ways that she had of cursing people. The most common was simply to cast heretics out of The Family and thus cancel the spiritual protection provided by their initiation. Any such person was cursed spiritually as well as physically. Not only would they die of cancer or something else painful, but they would also go to Hell. I told Helen and Erica that I couldn't talk to the police.

In the end Helen tricked me into it. She invited Anna, Andrea and myself to lunch at her place and after lunch two nice young women arrived. After I was introduced to them Helen told me they

The raid

were police officers from the Community Policing Squad (CPS). Believing what I did about police I could not believe how nice they were; they seemed so genuinely concerned. Without trying to pressure us to say anything they began to talk to us about Uptop, and soon I felt at ease. Gradually I began to feel I could trust them. The spectre of what was still happening to Cassandra and Stephen haunted my conscience. I finally decided to take action.

We had a couple of meetings with the two police officers, and eventually I agreed to make a statement. That first statement was qualified at frequent intervals with affirmations of my belief in Anne as I carefully tried not to condemn her openly. It was a short statement, eight pages in all, outlining our daily routine and common punishments. Certainly I never conceived of the train of events it would unleash. Convinced of Anne's supreme power, I thought the most the police would be able to do was go in and warn the Aunties to stop the abuse. I never realised everyone would be taken from Uptop until the day that it happened.

There were several meetings with doctors, child psychiatrists, social workers and police (with the District Support Group or DSG, the Drug Squad and regular uniformed police as well as our new-found friends from the CPS). It was at one of these meetings that I first met Doctor Edward Ogden, who worked with the police as a medical officer and was assigned to our case. I remember little of what was discussed during those meetings. I think we were required to give geographical details about Uptop and describe what we thought the reactions of the kids might be when the police burst into the house. The police decided that a raid would take place at 6.30 a.m. when the children would all be downstairs doing Hatha yoga and the adults all upstairs. The rigid routine made it easy to predict where everyone would be.

Friday, 14 August 1987: the day of the raid. The day that changed all our lives irrevocably. A day that is forever burned upon our memories, for nothing in our world would ever be the same again, and after that day we could never go back.

Helen drove Anna, Andrea and me down to Nunawading police station at 4 a.m. There we met the team of police who would be going up to Eildon on the raid. All together there were three busloads of police. Overkill, perhaps – which is what the police were accused of later – as we knew the Aunties were unarmed. The DSG, however, was just there to surround the property and prevent any escape. It has to be remembered that we children had been drilled in evasion from police, and it was feared the Aunties would try to smuggle out some of the kids via the lake.

The three of us – Andrea, Anna and I – sat in the last bus with Ed Ogden and the policewomen we knew. Helen was with other members of the police in squad cars in front. We were there mainly to reassure the other children because everyone knew they would be shocked and scared, too distrustful of strangers to be reassured by them. It was hoped that they would believe the truth when they heard it from us.

We arrived Uptop exactly as scheduled. The DSG surrounded the property and the remaining police divided into two groups. One group went down the hill and around to the back of the house, as we knew the back door would not be locked and the children would all be downstairs in a room just opposite that door. The others went to the front verandah and knocked on the main door; some also covered other doors that led out of the house.

I don't remember many details of the raid. I was too terrified and too devastated by the children's reaction to me when we arrived. I knew they'd been told I was a traitor, and now they thought they were experiencing proof of me selling them to the police, who would torture and kill them. When Julieanne saw the sledge-hammer the police jokingly referred to as their 'door key' she screamed, 'Is that what you are going to beat us up with?'. It must have seemed worse than the three-cornered cane or metre ruler! The children were hysterical. Bill was there and Julieanne clung to him, yelling hysterically until the police prised her loose. Annette cried over and over for her favourite belongings. David just sat there frozen, every now and then saying 'How could you?' to me and accusing me of betraying our parents. Aunty Helen kept saying to the children, 'We were going to have a really fun day today'.

All the children were crying and shaking with fear. I was looking everywhere for one of the cats because one of the children had said 'I'm not going without my cat'. Bill called me Judas and said it was bad enough taking his children but now I was taking his animals. That statement shouldn't have surprised me. I always thought he loved his little dog, Dinky, more than us kids.

It was only having Ed Ogden standing right behind me that gave me the courage to continue gathering the kids' belongings. My automatic reaction was still to cower in Bill's presence, and I expected him to attack me despite all the police. Annette refused to leave without her gloves and her torch, so I went to look for them. It was dreadful, with all the junk there, trying to find exactly what she wanted. Stephen was okay because the police let him look at their radio and he liked that because of his fascination with electronic gadgets. In the planning of the raid we had been worried that he might have a temper tantrum or an epileptic fit and be a problem to reassure.

Once we got all the children in the bus they calmed down. I'd brought some chocolate along and that helped to settle them. Before going to Melbourne we stopped off at the Eildon police station and, after being wary at first, the children became more relaxed. The police were terrific and the kids soon trusted them. It was remarkable how quickly the kids changed. After about an hour they settled down and began talking freely about life at Uptop. Once over their initial fear and alarm, the kids listened to us, and I think the genuine concern and caring of the people around them helped.

About half-way down to Melbourne we stopped in Lilydale at a place called Kids in Care for a huge brunch. It had all sorts of delicious food, half of which we'd never seen before, and we could have as much of it as we could eat. This, too, helped to break the fear. It was simple to win us over by feeding us and giving us some affection for we were starving for both.

I don't think any of us believed that we were leaving Uptop for good. We were unable to comprehend the enormity of the situation. I know I did not understand that the police had so much power: I thought once Anne swung her forces into action, no one – not even all the police in the world – could stand against her.

I remember Ben turning around to Ed and saying, 'I didn't think *anyone* was higher up than Mummy and Daddy'.

'Believe me, there are lots of people more powerful than them', I recall Ed saying in reply.

Although I was pleased that the children were starting to open up about Eildon and talk about how bad life had been there, and that they were appearing less traumatised by the raid, I felt that I was doomed. The accusations of the kids had struck home: I knew I was a traitor and therefore accursed. At that moment I resigned myself to losing my life.

Unbeknown to us, at the same time as the Uptop raid, police had also raided several of the houses in the Dandenongs, including Winberra and Crowther. At Crowther they found twelve LSD tablets in Anne's bedroom. From Uptop they took out several large bags of restricted schedule drugs, drugs that had been prescribed by cult doctors for the Aunties but were actually fed to us. They and other prescribed tranquillisers had been the major means of controlling our lives for all those years. The drugs were never used in charges against Anne or the Aunties. In fact, they mysteriously disappeared from police custody not long after the raid. Apparently this is not unusual, but looking back now it is an incident that seemed to set the scene for the rest of the police investigation into the cult.

CHAPTER 14

Aftermath

That August day in 1987 was the day when life for us actually started. It feels as if I never truly existed as a human being before that. I lived in what now seems somewhat of a dream, a fiendish game in which the rules were thought to be known but were always changing faster than I could follow – a dangerous world of constant uncertainty and subliminal terror.

Even before the raid, I had made it very clear to the caseworkers how important I thought it was that we kids stay together, and they found the unique solution of putting us all in one unit at Allambie. Allambie was at that time a State government reception centre used to house temporarily children under the age of 14 seen to be at risk of either committing criminal offences or of being physically or psychologically abused. Community Services Victoria (CSV) was in control of us there. Allambie was in Box Hill, and no longer exists as such. There were about a hundred children when we lived there, all waiting for court cases or for more permanent placement.

If the authorities at Allambie had not extended themselves and agreed to the unusual situation of housing us all, we would have been split up because most of us were much older than 14, and the system did not generally cope with such a large family group. Perhaps some of the younger children would have been put into

Allambie but the older girls would have gone to Winlaton and the boys to Turana, despite the fact that these were correctional facilities, generally accommodating street-kids or young criminals. It would have been a disaster for us, in the delicate psychological state we were in, if we had been separated. I am very thankful that we were allowed to stay together in those early days. I am convinced that, without each other's support, the relative isolation of a secure unit just for us, and the intensive care of the Allambie staff assigned to look after us, we would not have made it.

The time at Allambie was a period of great change and turmoil, but also of great excitement and discovery. For the first time in our lives we were allowed to be kids, with no punishment, restrictions or censorship. The day after we arrived, David crept into the kitchen. I followed him. Some of the staff were sitting around and saw him looking at the fridge. 'You can open it', they said. The fridge was packed full of delicious and previously forbidden food — what we had called 'Aunty food'. 'You can have anything you want from in there', someone said. I will never forget the look on David's face as he gazed into that fridge and realised he was free.

I also remember watching David the first time he got on a bike. There were many firsts like this, and it was wonderful to see the joy on the faces of my younger brothers and sisters. They were finally experiencing the happiness that comes from ordinary things, the things normal kids take for granted: being allowed to go for a swim, to use the playground equipment, to make a noise if they wanted. They discovered pocket money and going into a shop to buy lollies. The smaller ones gorged themselves on lollies for the first few weeks. They were finally being allowed to eat what they liked when they liked. On our first morning we discovered Coco Pops!

We at long last experienced the joy of rolling down a grassy hill, visiting Luna Park and the beach, watching cartoons on television in the morning, picnics, riding on Puffing Billy, shopping in the city. We caught up on all the celebrations we had missed by having heaps of birthday parties at Allambie, with balloons and streamers, cakes and chocolates and lollies. And finally we had grown-ups around us who cared for us and took an interest in us.

I am not saying that everything went smoothly for the Allambie staff. Although the majority of them were loving, caring and warm human beings who were very good at working with disturbed kids, they nevertheless had to come to terms with all that they were learning about our background and they had to get over the hurdle of viewing us as freaks, with our strange habits and identical blond hair. But we adapted incredibly quickly, and once they got to know us many close relationships were established. In fact, in a couple of weeks we became closer to some of the staff and police than we ever had been to any of the Aunties.

The first few weeks at Allambie were frantic. The story was all over the media and a crowd of reporters surged around the gates, trying all sorts of novel ways of getting to speak to us or to someone about us. So-called experts sprang up on radio and television programmes overnight, purporting to know us and describing what supposedly went on at Uptop. Of course, no one knew anything at that stage apart from what a few ex-cult members had said in previous interviews, so what was being reported about us and our lives was wildly off-beam. It might have been funny to sit before the television and listen to a totally wrong yet salacious account of what we looked like, from a private detective none of us had ever seen or heard of before, who had appointed herself an expert on the subject. She said that she had gone up to Lake Eildon when we were young and exposed her breasts to entice us to come down to the water's edge. Unfortunately we were too close to our experience to find it funny at the time.

Since our early experiences at the Dandenong Festival, we had always believed we were freaks so the public attention we received did not surprise us deeply. Anne had raised us as a scientific experiment, and we had been taught to believe that we were not like everyone else. Now here was the whole world saying so. But we stayed quiet. The last thing any of us wanted to do was talk to the media, even though we were angry at the inaccuracies. We were also in the middle of the court cases for protection applications, which would see us formally taken from the custody of Anne and Bill on the grounds of physical, emotional and psychological danger, and put in the care of the State.

The two youngest children, Cassandra and David, started to grow at a rapid rate. Cassandra, although she was probably about 12 years of age at that time, was the size of a 5-year-old. She was under 120 centimetres tall and weighed under 20 kilograms. With her blonde hair and pigtails, she looked like a small child. She, and to a lesser degree David, was suffering from what in medical terms is known as 'psychosocial short stature'. This is a condition of failed growth, which occurs when children have been so psychologically or physically harassed during their development that they fail to produce the growth hormone required for normal growth. As soon as such children get out of their poor environment, they start to produce growth hormone in the normal amounts. Cassandra, from being 12 centimetres shorter than most children of her age when we left Eildon, grew a massive 11 centimetres in that first year, with a spurt that put her rate of growth off the charts. To achieve this growth velocity she received no other treatment than re-establishment in a normal community – no pills or potions, and no intervention apart from care and affection and a normal diet.

The bleach started to grow out of the kids' hair. Some even had their hair dyed black within a week or so of being at Allambie. No one wanted to be a blond freak from a bizarre cult. Even today, every one of us tries to hide from what we were, to deny the reality of our past, because it is not compatible with surviving and adapting to the present.

The younger ones started to cultivate Australian accents, for we still stood out with our plum-in-the-mouth vowels and quaint figures of speech. The thing we wanted most passionately in the world was to blend in and be normal. We were sick of being different. The children wanted to fit in at school. They changed their names and denied being Hamilton-Byrnes, even when challenged.

To this day, a number of years after leaving the cult, I am the only one who retains that surname.

I keep the name Hamilton-Byrne for complicated reasons. First, I keep it because it is my name and to change it would be, for me, to admit in some kind of a way that the cult had won. I don't want to change my name just because now it's no longer acceptable to be a Hamilton-Byrne. The cult changed my name twice when I was small as well as my birth date and age. In 1984, when I stopped being Andrée and became Sarah, I felt in a strange way that I was somebody. I finally felt I had an identity: a name, an age, a birth date and a place in the family as one of triplets. To change my name again would be like saying the cult can still force me to hide myself. I know I've probably made it harder for myself by keeping it, but I am not yet ready to change. To change also would be to deny my past, which is me and part of what I am about. I can never totally ignore it, never run away from it – I am a Hamilton-Byrne with all that entails.

As I mentioned earlier, only some of the children managed to survive at school. The younger ones were the luckiest because they were young enough to have the capacity to adapt to the school system. I know I would not have coped at school. Luckily at Allambie I was able to continue with Year Twelve through correspondence. I used to go up to an abandoned floor and try to study in the relative quiet.

The police were at Allambie nearly every day, interviewing us. Things were not always easy for the children: the vast changes took their toll psychologically, and here the system let us down a bit. Before the raid, the authorities had agreed that there needed to be intensive individual counselling and debriefing for all of us. This never happened, although the authorities did bring in a psychologist who saw us for group counselling – something that, if they had thought about it, they would have realised was inevitably going to fail. We were children brought up to distrust everyone, even each other. We were hardly going to talk in a group situation about how we felt to a stranger, no matter how well-intentioned.

As well, I don't think we ourselves knew what we felt in those early days. People who knew us then say we had the emotional capacity of 2-year-olds. We couldn't define our own feelings, or realise that we were having them, let alone discuss them with others. We didn't even know that people and especially children, from whom shows of emotion had been forbidden, had feelings. Despite learning to trust a little, we were still afraid of adults. The staff at Allambie were surprised that whenever an adult approached us we would, despite ourselves, cower and cover our faces with an arm to protect our heads. It was a reflex, conditioned by years of expecting to be hit by every adult we knew. It has taken a very long time for us to recover from this basic distrust and suspicion; I think for some it continues. Counsellors and social workers never helped in this regard. It was only through finding friendship and love outside the welfare system that individually we learnt to become human and found the secret of happiness in the outside world.

I could not handle things at Allambie. I had resolved to support the other children to the best of my ability, but to a large degree I was useless. I had too many problems of my own. Thinking I was doomed, caught up in my fantasies of being the victim of The Family's revenge and retribution, I stopped eating and drinking. I spent my days hidden in the upstairs area, ostensibly studying, but really in a daze.

Edward Ogden, the police surgeon who had been on the raid, visited us from time to time. He had befriended some of us, and we were very fond of him, as we were of the policewomen from the CPS, who had kept in touch. We craved attention and affection from whoever was able to give it. We were exhausting to be around in those days: the need for love and warmth within us was so huge that it scared off quite a few people. It caused some angst for the case-workers; they had their notions of professional boundaries, which some were tempted to cross when they came into contact with us. I am grateful to those who were brave enough to weather the criticism of their peers and extend themselves to us on a personal level, for it was to them that we owed our psychological survival. If people had merely handled us 'professionally', without demonstrating to us that they loved us, we would never have grown enough to get free of the legacy of Uptop.

On one of his visits, Ed extended an invitation to us to come to his general practice to talk and receive counselling. For some reason I went: I suppose I thought I had nothing to lose for I imagined that I would die anyway, but I felt a great need to communicate with someone and Ed seemed kind and genuine. He was probably the first person outside the cult, apart from Erica, with whom I was able to form any sort of relationship on an emotional level. I was still very wary of people and didn't think that I could trust anyone. There seemed too much to do, all the other kids to think about. I started to talk to Ed and the words just kept coming. Although I think Ed, Erica and Marie Mohr – of whom I will talk later – are remarkably special people in their own right, I also think that to a degree they were special for me because they were the first kind people who were willing to listen when I was finally ready to talk.

The hunger inside me to tell someone about my confusion and my desperation was intense. Ed sat there, listened, and didn't judge. It was amazing to me at the time to find that I could relate to an adult on that level. I told him how I thought I was cursed by the Master because I had betrayed The Family. I said I thought I was going to die. I was ready for it, I told Ed. I also said I hadn't thought it would all come to this. I thought the police would just go to Uptop and tell the Aunties to straighten out their act. I hadn't thought they'd actually take the kids out of there. If I'd known that, I doubt whether I'd have gone along with it. I told him I hadn't really wanted to betray Anne. I thought the outside world wasn't as good as I'd been led to believe either. It was necessary to have relationships with everyone. I had all these emotions, feelings I hadn't been allowed at Uptop, and they were swamping me.

I felt a huge gap in my chest. The place where all the years of nurturing should have gone was a void. I felt unable to behave like a normal person because I knew I wasn't one. I couldn't talk to people, I couldn't make small talk, I didn't know where to look half the time. I had seldom been spoken to as an individual in my own right and here were people expecting me to know what to do. Well, I *didn't* know what to do.

Ed seemed to be the only person who sensed how close to the edge I was at that dreadful time, the only person who wanted to listen to me, who wanted to try to understand what I was going through, and I thank him for taking a chance on me, despite the disapproval of others. I found myself regularly going out to his general practice. I had confided in no one at Allambie. They didn't even know I was starving myself although, at the time I went to see Ed, I was close to renal failure through not drinking and was hallucinating intensely. He ended up taking me in to live with his family in Kalorama, and I stayed there for about six weeks. I was being labelled schizophrenic by the social workers, and he alone thought I would be all right.

It made all the difference to me to know that at least one person believed in me. It was only later that I found out that he had risked professional censure by taking me into his own home. I am forever grateful for his faith in me because I firmly believe that without him I would be dead several times over. There, supported by and thanks to his patience and love, I fought to survive. I fought my own crazy conviction that I was accursed and doomed to die. I fought the irrational terrors and fears that were consuming me and making me totally dysfunctional. I fought what I thought at the time was the power of my guru punishing me, and what I know now was only the power of my own mind that I ascribed to Anne. Eventually I won the battle, or I would not be here now to tell the tale, but it was a long struggle and for many weeks I was completely out of it – unaware of the outside world, consumed by my inner turmoil.

Ed became the father I had never had and a life-long friend. I think it's partly because of him I achieved the stability required to study Medicine successfully. I feel that I owe to him a lot of what I have now achieved and have now become.

I was eventually able to study again, and stayed mainly at Ed's until the end of my HSC. He applied for me to do the end of year exams at Montrose High rather than in the city because I'd become severely agoraphobic and it was a huge effort for me to go outside the house. Ed suggested I apply for Medicine at Melbourne University. Having never sat external exams before, I had no idea how I would do and, seeing no future, I had not ever thought of a career. I suppose if it had been up to me I would have put down 'nursing' as my intended vocation as that is what the girls were supposed to do according to cult doctrine.

I went back to Allambie in late November 1987. The court cases for the protection applications, although expected to run for weeks, ended up going only for days, as Anne and Bill did not contest them. Although they said publicly that they would fight bitterly for us children, the threat of unwanted publicity and exposure, through evidence that would have been presented if the cases had been contested, caused them to let us go without a fight. That hurt, too, in a way, although it seems incongruous; we still wanted to believe that they loved us, and once again they showed us how little we meant.

In any case, the children had all stated firmly that they did not want to go back, and vividly described some of the horrors of Uptop in police statements. All of our stories were similar and rang true. The protection applications taken out by the police were thus upheld, and the younger children were taken into custody as official wards of the state, thus guaranteeing them social and financial support until they were of age.

During the court cases, we discovered our true identities. Instead of the usual six-year waiting list, and because the police were desperate to find out who we all were, the CSV's adoption information service placed us at the top of the list and unravelled the rather convoluted documentation for nearly all of us, in a matter of only six weeks. I say nearly all of us. They could not find out who Cassandra was, nor could they retrieve papers for Benjamin and David because these two boys had been born to cult members and thus were without documentation.

Anne to this day maintains she is Cassandra's real mother. But this is not possible. She would have been 54 years old at the time of the birth, and she would have had to perform the miracle of giving birth after a hysterectomy. Quite a feat, even for a divine Master!

We think we know who Cassandra's parents are; at least we are fairly sure about her father. She even has, we believe, two half-sisters within the cult. But her parents are still staunch cult members and would never come forward, so, sadly, she is denied the truth.

From a vicious and cowardly phone call he received from his mother, Benjamin discovered she was an inner core cult member and one of the Aunties whom we knew. This woman reviled, attacked and disowned him by telephone, at that time in his life when he was in so much need of love and security. Once again, in my eyes the cruelty of the regime we had left was amply demonstrated.

Being told that Anne and Bill were not our real parents was very difficult to accept initially. When I was growing up I had clung fiercely to the belief that, despite everything, Anne must love me because I was her own flesh and blood. Despite her poor performance as a parent, she was after all the Master and it was a privilege to be related to her. It was something that made me special, closer to the Master than even the longest-serving cult members: I was one of the guru's offspring. I had thought that, despite everything that had happened, she loved me because everyone loves their kids. No matter what they do or say, everyone loves their kids. This is what I had believed. It had got me through all those years. The shattering of that illusion was bitter.

The court days were hard on everyone. At one stage, as Benjamin spoke eloquently about how he felt to be free, everyone in the courtroom was weeping: police, Salvation Army people, caseworkers, even the judge was wiping his nose and eyes. Benjamin said that, in the short time we had been out, we had experienced more love than in all the years of broken promises and deceit and being told that we were loved – but never shown it.

All this time we had not spoken to the media. But then Anne, who was still in the United States, and Bill went public (although Bill slipped out of Australia before the story broke so he could not be charged by the police for releasing photographs identifying the younger children, who were now wards of state). We once again felt betrayed, because Bill had given us an assurance that there would be no more lies and that he was sorry for what he had done. We, desperate to believe him, had accepted this. So we felt both angry and sad when we read, in stark black and white and in an exclusive series of articles by a journalist called Ben Hills – someone Bill said was an old friend – the lies that Anne and Bill now produced to defend themselves. They said that they had never given us drugs, that they had never abused us. They said that they only took us in because we were unwanted by anyone else: that we were children with great physical or behavioural problems, from 'the scrap-heap of society'.

'Would you send a dog back to the pound?', they said in justification for adopting us. We knew already that we were considered lower than dogs in their eyes.

Ben Hills went on television to say that Anne and Bill were 'innocent victims of a modern day witch-hunt' and that we were all retarded. All of the kids were enraged. That Anne and Bill now lied to justify what they had done to us was very hard to bear. Finally, I felt compelled to say something to rebut these lies, and I wrote an article for the *Australian* and Anna and I got in touch with Marie Mohr from the Channel Nine programme *A Current Affair*.

I met Marie Mohr in late 1987. At that time I was dividing my time between Allambie and Ed's place. Due to the Children's Court injunctions protecting the privacy of wards of state and to our own wish for privacy, we had not had anything to do with the media during the court cases. This was despite the fact that all sorts of people and self-appointed experts on the cases seemed to be writing and saying anything they felt like about us.

Edward Ogden was horrified by our treatment in the media. He was, I felt at the time, the only one who understood us. Although I didn't know it then, when Marie Mohr rang him to talk about the cases, he felt she would understand us better than most journalists. She had been on the story since 1985 and knew quite a lot of the background.

I met Marie at Ed's place one night. She remembers that I didn't look at her at first, though I don't remember that. She seemed nice, open and honest, and full of life and laughter: not at all how I had envisaged a dreaded 'member of the media'. I started to trust Marie. Finally I introduced her to the other kids. Soon she became friends with us all. She was always straight with us, often ringing to let us know when something was going on with the cases.

Like many who got to know us, Marie was fierce about getting justice for us. But in May 1988 we were dealt a cruel blow. We were told by the CPS police that due to the statutory limitation of twelve months from the date of abuse, the authorities were unable to proceed with prosecuting members of The Family for what they had done to us. We were devastated. I remember the date, 17 May, well because we were all so upset: it seemed these people would get off scot-free for all those years of systematic child abuse. It is true that some of the Aunties were going through the courts at this time, charged with social security fraud and other offences, and in fact convictions were made and some went to prison. Needless to say, we couldn't believe that no one would be charged for child abuse. We railed at the irony and injustice of it. We decided to go public again, to let people know what had happened and perhaps to shame the authorities into taking action.

Four of us did a story for *A Current Affair* and there was a bit of a media drive to get the authorities to do something. It was finally agreed to establish a police inquiry, and a task force was

Aftermath

established, which came to be called Operation Forest.

In July 1989 I went to England with Marie to try to get in touch with Timothy and Luke, the boys I'd believed were my triplet brothers. I wanted them to know what was going on in Australia and to tell them about their real identities. They had been at Broom Farm at the time of the raid, and I was sure that they wouldn't have been told the truth about our rescue. I was sure they still believed themselves to be Hamilton-Byrnes.

I also just wanted to see them again. For most of my life I had believed that they were my brothers and I loved them. I was worried about them, too, still stuck over there under Anne's control, never having had the chance that we had to make their own judgements about the outside world, to experience what life was like away from the cult. Although they had attended school in England, their understanding of reality was still determined by what Anne said, and they hadn't had a chance to challenge that reality because they weren't in possession of any of the facts.

Marie and I found Luke and Timothy, as we'd hoped, in a pub near Broom Farm, the same pub where I had first started drinking as a teenager with my brothers when I was last in England in 1986. We spent nearly a week talking to them, trying to tell them the truth about their lives, trying to get them to believe us. It was an almost impossible task. They had been told by Anne that I had betrayed her, and they were also not about to trust Marie, whom they believed was out to destroy their mother.

Timothy and Luke at that time were the most disturbed teenagers I've ever seen. I had thought their lives might be miserable because they were not equipped to cope with adult life, but what I found was worse than I could ever have imagined. Luke was overtly suicidal. Timothy told us that his brother had stepped out in front of a bus on one occasion, and that he would jump out of windows to try and hurt or kill himself; it seemed only a matter of time before he was successful. He was drunk or drugged most of the time as a means of escape from reality. Timothy himself was in trouble. Anne had demanded he keep himself and he was in thousands of pounds of debt and living a life on the run from his many creditors, doing night-time flits from the hovels he lived in to avoid paying the rent. He was dressed practically in rags and had no money at all. Neither of them was able to form a significant relationship with anyone else. They were lonely, depressed wrecks.

Marie and I talked and talked to them, emotionally, rationally, we tried everything. I remember how desperately sad I felt when I saw how they were suffering; how I longed to get through to them and be able to help them in their unhappiness. I debated with them, I tried to comfort them, I attempted to show them there was a better world than the one we'd grown up in. I tried to get them to be brave, to break the wretched code of 'Unseen, Unheard, Unknown'. They agreed that we had been beaten and treated badly, but staunchly defended Anne and Bill's right to treat us like that, saying that the discipline was deserved because we were difficult kids. Initially, they thought that all the documentation we had brought concerning their adoptions, and showing that they were not Anne's children, were forgeries. When they finally accepted the truth about their parentage, they rationalised it by saying that Anne knew best and that is why she had never told us who we were.

They both said they never trusted anyone and that was how they survived. It was heart wrenching for me to hear this and to know that I was helpless to do anything for them unless they wanted me to. It reminded me of myself a year earlier; of standing on a divide with the future before me and the past behind. Which should I choose? Although you can be guided by those around you, in the end you have to make the decision yourself.

By the end of the week, Marie and I had persuaded Timothy to come back to Australia on a trial basis. Luke still desperately wanted to be loved by Anne and did not want to be seen betraying her. He would not countenance the idea of leaving England, but at least I think we sparked in him an interest in finding out who his real parents were, and hopefully we stimulated him to start asking questions of the system and to accept no longer everything blindly on faith.

Timothy had many troubles adapting to life in Australia outside the cult, as we all did at first. For a while he worked for Channel Nine. He lived with us kids, then he spent time in the Dandenongs with The Family. We didn't push him or give him ultimatums, we just tried to show him we loved him. He had agreed to come back with us on the condition that he have a return ticket and the freedom to go back to England if and when he wanted, and that we not try to force him to make up his mind about who was right or wrong or to say anything against Anne. He was still maintaining publicly that Anne and Bill were the best, most loving people in the world, although in private he would often agree with us that this was not so. Despite us trying to show him that the outside world was not such a bad place and that we loved him, eventually decided to cast in his lot with the cult again. He returned to the Dandenongs. While his reasons for going back were probably quite complex, and probably mainly to do with not wanting to lose Anne's approval, when he left he only admitted to having an interest in her money.

At least now I can console myself that, unlike when he was trapped in England with no access to any information other than the cult's version of events, he was making a reasonably informed decision. He knew what Anne and Bill were about, he was no longer an innocent victim living in ignorance and trapped in the system. It became his choice to return. I do not agree with his choice, and I think he is totally ignoring large slabs of reality and living in a fairytale world, where he has convinced himself that our past never happened and that Anne and Bill are innocent, persecuted and in need of support and that we others have sold out to the outside world. This is the version of reality that is psychologically easiest for him to accept at present. I still care for him deeply, but I no longer feel he needs saving. He can now decide for himself which side his bread is buttered on.

CHAPTER 15

Answers to old questions

In late 1988 I finally met my mother. My feelings were very mixed about this meeting. Ever since I had found out that I was adopted a few months before, I had fantasised about what she would be like. I had looked at women in the train, in the bus, in the street, and wondered if they were my mother. I had gazed out the window to the hills sometimes and wondered where she was and what she was doing. Not knowing the circumstances surrounding my birth, I had wondered what sort of woman would give me up to a cult like The Family. I hoped like mad that she did not belong to the cult.

Despite some initial reluctance, I had been determined to find my parents. I did fear the reality of meeting my mother. Some of the other children had met their parents and in most cases the relationship had not worked out as they had hoped. I did a paper on this when I began studying Medicine and found it was not unusual that few children got on with their biological mothers. Apparently it is common for adopted people to feel disappointed when they meet their birth mothers.

I put off meeting my mother, partly because, despite everything, I did not want to give up the fantasy of Anne as my mother. Eventually, however, my curiosity got the better of me and, with Ed acting as a facilitator, we arranged to meet in Ed's rooms.

My mother was only 16 years old when I was born, my father only a year older. She lived in Belgrave, a suburb in the Dandenong Ranges, not 3 kilometres from Ferny Creek. Before she became pregnant at 15, my mother had been attending the local high school. I found that my mother was a beautiful young naturopath, successful and highly intelligent, and that all these years she had been waiting for my return, never dreaming where I had ended up. I found I had a new little sister, only a year old. Now, a number of years later, I have three baby sisters.

My mother had naively assumed that I would come looking for her once I came of age, not knowing about the six-year waiting period at Adoptions. That is one of the changes brought about by our cases. Many smaller agencies have sprung up, and the waiting time is now only a few months. Also thanks to our cases, the adoption laws have been tightened up. So, although I sometimes think that no one has learnt anything from what happened to us and that society and the legal system does not care how we suffered, some small good has come from our experience.

My relationship with my mother was slow to develop. She was sensible enough not to push me and to allow us gradually to get to know each other at a pace largely determined by me. Once she got over the guilt that she felt, unreasonably, for where I had been, our friendship blossomed. We have a friendship now like that of sisters, for after all she is only fifteen years older than I am. However, we will never retrieve what is forever lost to me: a mother–daughter relationship.

The tears are running uncontrollably down my face and I am filled with feelings of sadness as I write this for, seeing her bring up my three gorgeous sisters, I understand more than ever just what it was that I missed in my childhood. Not having the love of a mother was the hardest thing to bear. Not having a breast to suckle on as a baby, not having the unconditional warmth and affection that is normally unequivocally bestowed on infants in a family: that is what leaves an ache in me. It is a pain that will never go away, no matter how well I adapt to this outside world.

It was unnecessary for Anne to be so cruel to us. And now that I know that my mother would gladly have kept me and brought me up, and that if it wasn't for the social pressure and the deceit of the cult I could have grown up with her, I weep for the childhood I never had.

My baby sisters will never know this pain. I see my mother shower them with love and affection, with cuddles and smiles. They accept it as their right, and it is indeed the natural right of every child, a right that was denied the children of The Family. We had no hugs and tenderness, no cuddles and smiles as small children, we had no mother or caring figure to lavish upon us unconditional love and affection. Our interactions with adults were filled with fear and pain. The mottos that ruled our lives were 'You can't murder a bum', and 'A belting a day keeps evil away'. The mother that we loved so much was the sort of woman who held up a child by its ankles in front of an admiring group of followers to show them 'the best way to belt a child', the sort of woman who would ask someone to hold up the phone while a child was getting belted so that she could 'hear the screams'. We were deprived of almost everything normal children take for granted. I think the withholding of love is the worst thing The Family did to us and has had the most lasting effect. I believe to deny a child love is to deny its existence as a human being.

When my mother was a teenager her two passions were Jesus and her boyfriend. She'd become a devout Christian a year before she had me, after seeing a Billy Graham film at a Youth for Christ rally in Melbourne. She considered herself 'born again' and was an active member of the local Baptist youth group. She had taken part in rallies in the city square with 'long-haired peace freaks playing guitars and singing about Jesus'.

Her boyfriend, my father, whom she later married (and divorced), was also a Christian. They met at a mod dance in 1967 and became inseparable. They went to the same high school and would rush to meet each other at recess. They had lots of friends, they swam competitively, they were fit and tanned and their hair was made fair by the sun. My mother had a friendship ring from her boyfriend and they planned, one day, to marry. They were madly in love. And, like all the teenagers they knew, they petted heavily. They knew little about sex apart from the biological facts. They listened to the Beatles and the Stones, dressed like hippies and considered themselves 'cool'. They had no idea of the intricacies of sex. They loved each other with a painful passion. They believed that they never went 'all the way'; nevertheless in church they repented of what they did do. My mother was as surprised as everyone else to discover that she was nearly four months pregnant. She was on holidays at Ocean Grove with her best friend's family. Her friend's mother took her to see Doctor G. in Ocean Grove. He was sympathetic, but his eyebrows shot up when she said she hadn't done anything and couldn't be pregnant.

From then on her life became a blur of shame and disgrace. It was decided by her family that she should be sent away. In those days Belgrave was a very close-knit and gossip-ridden community. My mother didn't go back to school and the story was put about that she was going off to stay with a grandmother in Queensland for a few months. Her family and friends were sworn to secrecy. My mother's sixteenth birthday party in February 1969 was really a farewell to the life and friends she'd known. She put on a brave face and smiled, pretending to be elated about going to Queensland. In fact she left for Hopper's Crossing, near Werribee, a few days later.

Her parents had decided before she left Belgrave that she should visit a local doctor. She didn't want to see the family doctor because she was ashamed to face him. It was suggested that she go to the Upwey surgery where my father's mother worked part-time. A new female doctor had joined the practice, and it was thought that she would be more sympathetic. Her name was Doctor Beryl Hubble. Her husband, Trevor, was my mother's family dentist. Doctor Hubble seemed very kind when my mother first saw her. She seemed sincere, listened sympathetically to my mother's protested innocence and prescribed some iron.

Beryl Hubble at that time was a tall, energetic woman in early middle age. She was modern. She knew how to talk to young people. My mother trusted her implicitly. She described what my mother's pitiful fate would be if she kept the child, and talked glowingly about the wonderful life her child could have if adopted by a loving couple. She urged my mother to keep up her studies and to adopt the baby out. She inquired about the birthing arrangements that had been made and said she would send my mother's medical details to the delivering doctor, Doctor G., whom my mother had first visited in Ocean Grove.

What my mother didn't know until I escaped the cult was that Doctor Beryl Hubble was Raynor Johnson's daughter, and was acting for Anne all along. As a child I knew Doctor Hubble as a prominent member of The Family, and a trusted companion and confidante of Anne. By then she called herself Doctor Christine Fleming.

The next tearful months passed slowly for my mother. She was staying with friends of her parents. Hopper's Crossing, on the western outskirts of Melbourne, was a lonely, windswept place in those days, with only the new housing estates to break the monotony of the flat horizon. Her hosts were kind but she was ashamed of herself. She despaired for the future. She buried herself in a correspondence course, determined to vindicate herself, at least academically. She longed for her family's weekend visits or for the rare visit or letter from her boyfriend.

Her doctor during this time was a doctor in Altona, a gruff old chap who she remembers sneered with distaste every time he examined her. Towards the end of her term she took a flat in Ocean Grove with her mother. She wanted Doctor G. to attend the delivery. At the clinic she was told she'd be unable to see Doctor G. because he'd suffered a minor hear attack. She would see his uncle, Doctor C., who had been informed about the case by Doctor Hubble.

Doctor C. was an older man who seemed kind enough. He gave her the usual pep talk about putting this behind her and concentrating on her studies and about how much better off the child would be without her. She'd heard these words before in many forms and from many people.

Doctor C. recommended her to a gynaecologist named Doctor Kelso in Geelong, who would deliver the baby. My mother never thought to question this Doctor C.'s authority, though she remembers thinking it strange that, when she called in without an appointment one day, she was able to find Doctor G. at work in the surgery.

She went with her mother to see Doctor Kelso in Geelong. While they were there she was subjected to an extensive interview about her background and that of her boyfriend. The doctor quizzed her about the medical, social and academic records, sporting interests, hobbies, physical colouring and ethnic history of them both. My mother thought it intrusive and asked why he wanted so much information. She was told that it was to enable the doctor to determine the baby's weight and so be prepared for the delivery. She remembers thinking the answer was odd.

My mother was in Geelong again the following week visiting the office of a social worker, a Miss Farrow, who'd been recommended by Doctor Kelso. Miss Farrow said she'd been trying to arrange for the child's adoption to a professional couple recommended by Doctor Hubble. Miss Farrow said something could be done about the length of time on waiting lists for adoptive babies. My grandmother was keen for a quick adoption because she was concerned that a long waiting period could adversely affect the baby. My mother's own feelings were ambivalent. She was confused that everyone seemed to be making these decisions for her. She sat through another lecture on doing the right thing and then it was time to await the birth.

At Geelong Hospital when the time came, she was taken away, shaved, given an enema, put into a hospital gown and left alone for five hours. She was frightened and in a lot of pain. A woman in the next room was screaming but my mother was determined not to make any noise. She says she vowed no one would hear her utter a single cry. It was the only form of control over the circumstances that she could exercise; she was determined that they would not make her cry.

At about 3.30 a.m. Doctor Kelso was called in. My mother was given nitrous oxide. She remembers being told to push. By this stage she was flat on her back with her feet in stirrups. Suddenly they turned her head to the wall and put a pillow over her face. She felt she was splitting in half, then she heard a baby cry. She never saw me being born, just a shadow on the wall as I was pulled out. She was never allowed to hold or even see me.

The midwife took the baby from the room and the doctor stitched up my mother. No one spoke. She felt like a slab of meat. She was given an injection to 'calm you down'. After the sedative she felt the blood in her head singing. She felt she was floating near the ceiling. From this position she heard someone say very clearly 'We've lost her'. It was 5.15 a.m. on 8 July 1969.

Gradually she became aware of people fussing about her in a worried way and of the nurses' relief that she'd 'come back'. Eventually she sat up with a blinding headache and vomited until she retched bile. Her memory is of a hospital bed. It was late afternoon. She was alone. She could hear none of the screams of the previous night. It was very still. Finally she was told that she'd delivered a healthy 2950-gram girl. She was told that she was not allowed to see or name the baby for fear that it might lead to bonding. The baby was not mentioned again, except in reference to the adoption. She saw no other mothers and didn't hear a baby cry.

The doctor told her that the vomiting had been due to an allergic reaction to morphine and that she should avoid all opiates in the future. For years she believed this and even had the allergy stated on her driving licence. Now she believes that the doctor gave her an over-dose, possibly deliberately.

The days she spent at Geelong Hospital were a blur. Twice a day she was visited by either someone from the church or the social worker, who would urge her to sign the adoption papers. They told her the baby would not receive the proper attention until she signed. They badgered her and played on her guilt. She felt constantly drowsy but put it down to having just had the baby. Finally she signed the papers. She had been led to believe that she had no other option. No one ever mentioned the possibility of her keeping the baby and after four or five days the birth was beginning to seem like a dream to her. She felt that she had to get out of the hospital before she went mad, and she thought she couldn't leave until the papers were signed.

It wasn't until 1990, when the police unearthed my mother's medical records from a storehouse, that we found she'd been given Largactil during her stay at Geelong Hospital. Largactil is a major tranquilliser, once used in the treatment of high blood pressure during pregnancy. My mother has never had high blood pressure: the only effect of the drugs was to bomb her out. This meant she'd signed a legal document while she was tranquillised. She was never told she could change her mind. The police later found correspondence between Doctor Kelso and Doctor Hubble, letters discussing my mother's situation. On being informed that 'the mother' was being 'a bit unco-operative' about signing the adoption papers, Doctor Kelso was advised by Doctor Hubble to 'work' on her a bit harder. My mother signed the papers in the smallest handwriting she could manage. She told herself that one day her daughter would see this tiny signature and understand the reluctance she'd felt about giving her up. It was to be her only message to me for eighteen and a half years.

Part of the reason my mother had had her baby in Geelong was because Doctor Hubble had assured her that this would mean the baby would be adopted a long way away from Belgrave. One of my mother's worst fears was of looking into every pram and wondering if the child inside was her own. This dreadful feeling would be partially averted if she thought I was being brought up far away.

The fact is that Beryl Hubble herself adopted me and then handed me over to Anne. That year, 1969, was when Anne Hamilton-Byrne began collecting babies, babies that she could raise as her own, brain-washed from infancy. We were to be reared as a new generation of The Family, who would spread the word and convert people after the holocaust Anne was so sure would eventuate. She believed the cult would inherit Earth, after the inevitable massive explosion that would destroy most of the planet, and that we children in particular would be the future leaders of Earth.

Beryl Hubble continued to be my mother's family doctor for many years after my birth, and her husband continued as the family dentist. Not a word was breathed about me, and never did my mother suspect that these professionals, so trusted by her family, had taken her child and given her away to a cult. My mother knew nothing about The Family or about Anne Hamilton-Byrne and had no reason to distrust Doctor Hubble or to question her actions. I feel incredibly angry when I contemplate the level of deceit that Beryl Hubble perpetrated on my mother and her abuse of the doctor–patient relationship. My mother's parents, too, never knew what had become of me. I think Beryl Hubble's action all those years ago was viewed by the rest of the family as a relief. Getting pregnant at 15 was an outrageous scandal in the 1960s. There was no question of abortion because both my mother's and father's families were strict Christians. They were glad to get rid of the problem and pretended it had never happened.

In retrospect, my mother thinks Doctor Hubble viewed her pregnancy as full of potential for the cult from the moment they met. From Doctor Hubble's point of view, an off-spring from my parents – with their blond hair and athletic, intelligent and innocent characteristics – must have seemed perfect material for The Family. Later we discovered the average age of all the children's biological mothers was seventeen. They were largely coerced into giving up their babies by members of the cult. All reported that at the time they hadn't wanted to do it. There was a lot of guilt, and some had kept the existence of a child a secret from their subsequent partners. Many had families who knew nothing about the earlier child.

The sadness of it all still affects me. I find the act of refusing a woman the chance to hold her baby incredibly tragic. My mother didn't even know that I had the same dark red hair as my father. But sometimes the little things can console you. We both take some comfort from the knowledge that Sarah is one of the names she thought of for me.

CHAPTER 16

My journey to survival

We moved to the St John's Homes for Boys and Girls in Canterbury about Christmas 1987. This was an Anglican organisation that volunteered to have us. We still stayed together in one unit, and over a period of a month or so all the case-workers we knew at Allambie were exchanged for new people.

There were many problems with the stay at St John's. Unfortunately, due to our notoriety, I feel that we became political pawns and often the victims of other people's power games. I began to doubt whether our welfare was the first consideration of some of the people at St John's.

Far from the affection and warmth that we had experienced from the staff at Allambie, the whole concept and methods of the staff at St John's were completely different. The hierarchy at St John's believed it was important that staff remain aloof. The few staff who tried to befriend or comfort us were encouraged to leave. No affection was allowed; that was interpreted as a risk to 'professional boundaries'. At the same time, the St John's hierarchy actively tried to stop us making outside friends; new people were discredited. It was almost as if the St John's hierarchy was jealous that we could be close to outsiders and yet not trust its staff members to look after us. The staff were rude to the few people who had befriended us: to Ed and to Denise Whyte, a policewoman in the CPS involved in the initial raid, who had been a friend to us all since that dramatic turning point in our lives. They were rude to Sue, a friend of Denise, who had also befriended us, and to other members of the police who had a close relationship with us. They gave Marie Mohr a particularly hard time, and at one stage attempted to ban the children from going to visit her.

Some of the staff at St John's were especially vitriolic. And it wasn't just outsiders whom they accused of having untoward motives. They accused one of my brothers, with no foundation, of sexual intentions towards one of my sisters; and they accused two of their own staff who had befriended the children of having sexual motives. These people had done nothing to deserve these allegations. St John's set one brother against the rest, and even lied when they engaged a publicity agent for him without consulting the rest of us, denying the fact that they had done so.

They hired some cottage parents who were glaringly inappropriate and who later resigned. A lot of the other staff were insufficiently qualified or informed about us to properly look after us and address the issues related to our background that constantly arose.

Instead of supporting us in our decision to go public with our case, they constantly criticised our version of what had happened and held our stories up to derision. The St John's hierarchy tried to get us to pretend that Uptop had never happened; they did not tell new staff anything of our background and encouraged them not to pursue the details. The philosophy seemed to be, 'Don't talk about it and it will all go away'. Whenever we tried to explain our background to them, they accused us of being self-indulgent and of wanting sympathy. Indeed, it seemed as if some members of the hierarchy at St John's were openly hostile towards us and working against our wish to succeed in the outside world. I started to wonder if there was a covert link between St John's and the cult, but that is unlikely. I honestly think that some of the St John's staff were manipulative people, using us for their own ends.

There was little love lost between the CSV and St John's, and this was to the absolute detriment of effective communication between them. The CSV was supposed to have the ultimate responsibility for our welfare. St John's, at times, misled them about what was going on with us. For example, they secretly sought out and introduced one of my younger brothers, who was a ward of state at the time, to his natural mother. They forbade the boy to confide in us or tell the CSV. Eventually he let some of us know what he was doing and that St John's staff had told him not to tell any of us. At no time during these introductory meetings did they inform the CSV of their actions.

The CSV needed to be involved in finding our natural parents because there were inherent risks. It was not known how many of our natural parents were still involved with Anne. Not only that, the potential psychological ramifications were so great that it was something that should have been approached with great sensitivity and forethought, with the welfare of the child foremost in mind, and not carried out to meet anyone else's political or personal agenda. The finding of our parents was a delicate operation that I believe the people at St John's blundered into without regard for anyone.

In hindsight I think that one aspect of the problem that confronted our carers was that the welfare system, of which we had suddenly become a part, seldom dealt with children of our age and intellectual capacity. The workers were unused to children representing themselves and challenging decisions. We often argued for our rights with the hierarchy at St John's and refused to be manipulated by them. We rebelled against being told who we could or could not befriend. We had come a long way from Uptop, where we would merely have accepted such manipulation without question.

These are just a few sketchy examples of what went wrong at St John's: I am hesitant to supply more detail. I just want to say that life at St John's was at times very miserable, especially in the last few months that we were there, and I think this was unnecessary. I may just be bitter about what I perceived to be a lack of caring and compassion; I would be the first to admit that we were hard kids to look after. We had many problems in those early years. But there was a stark contrast between Allambie and St John's. At times, my experiences at St John's reawakened unpleasant memories of Uptop.

To my mind, the only good thing that eventuated from our stay at St John's was that we met a wonderful couple called Rachel and Tim, who were to become close friends and very supportive to several of the kids. We met this couple after our cottage parents left: they filled in as an interim measure until new staffing arrangements could be made. Tim and Rachel are people filled with a great zest and enjoyment of life, and they were able to show affection and open their home and their hearts to this group of children and young adults. In fact, two of the children are living with them at present, and they have been like surrogate parents to several of us over the last few years.

I started medical school at Melbourne University in 1988. Unfortunately, I had to defer half-way through that year. I got ill with glandular fever and, coupled with this, I was not coping psychologically. That year of 1988 would have to be close to the worst year of my life, rivalled only perhaps by 1987 and 1984. The only good thing about 1988 was the formation of a friendship with two wonderful women who became a primary source of strength and support for me over the next three or four years.

One was Denise Whyte, the policewoman in the CPS, and the other was Sue, a single mother of two teenagers, who shared a house with Denise. They took me under their wing and into their lives, and it was through their kindness and love that I survived this second very rough patch in my life, spending time in their warm and affectionate home, a place where I felt a lot more supported and wanted than I did at St John's.

University was an entirely alien environment for me. I had never experienced normal school life before. Still mildly agoraphobic, I was terrified sitting in a lecture theatre with 200 other people. I was scared of other people and miserably shy. I felt isolated and was often out of touch with reality. I frequently had LSD flashbacks, which made my life hell.

I could cope with the academic workload – in fact, immersing myself in study was a prime survival and escape mechanism in those days – but I could not cope with living. I did not want to be part of the outside world. I could not see how I could ever be happy. I was lonely and depressed and saw death as the only escape from an intolerable situation. I felt worthless as a human being and I believed I had failed at life.

At that time, having a firm belief in reincarnation, I accepted that death was not the end, and so it seemed a good solution to my misery and despair. Several times I tried to kill myself, sometimes almost subconsciously. I do not remember most of that year; I think I was constantly in a trance or a daze, not functioning on a rational level at all.

After my second serious suicide attempt, as a result of which I had ended up in the intensive care unit of Box Hill Hospital for several days, Ed and Denise, in desperation, admitted me to Larundel, one of Melbourne's major psychiatric hospitals. It does not make me proud to recount how low I sank at that time; I had given up on life and was wallowing in my own misery. I had let the cult beat me: I was unable to survive on my own. I was truly, despite everything, on my way to 'dying in the gutter', in Anne's memorable words.

Of course, no one at St John's seemed to know anything about my troubles at this time, or at least they never mentioned them. They did not seem to care. They resented my spending time at Denise and Sue's house, and accused me of abandoning the other kids. I did not want to tell the kids either about what I was going through. I did not want them to see that I was weak, that I could not cope. I believed they needed me to be a role model, and I desperately wanted to appear to them to be strong and capable, to show them that we could make it, despite our past.

I was the one who was supposed to be successful, and here I was failing. I think most of them still don't know to this day what went on. I am still ashamed of it, but I don't think there was anything I could have done to prevent my collapse at that point of my life. It needed to happen so I could move on – if I didn't succeed in destroying myself first.

I only had a short stay in Larundel. I was initially admitted, because of lack of beds, to North Eight, a locked ward for chronic psychotics. I was terrified in there. I cannot forget the screams of those people at night and being locked in with them knowing that I wasn't insane, but unsure how to prove it and where to go from there. I couldn't see any way out. It seemed that one of Anne's erstwhile predictions that I would 'end my days in a loony bin' had come true. I thought that I would never get out.

I knew that I was not mentally ill: it was merely that the ways I had learnt to adapt to mental stress, which had been so useful when under attack in the cult, were considered bizarre and inappropriate in this outside world. Rolling oneself into a catatonic ball was considered mad behaviour by society, as were the hallucinations and voices that were caused by my LSD flashbacks. I had to learn to control this behaviour or I would never adapt, and it was going to be up to my will-power to do this. Psychotropic drugs, I knew from the many years of having been force-fed them as a child, would not help the situation. They would just make me crazier and less able to control my mind. Spending time in a mental institution would merely teach me how to act demented.

However strange it may seem, being locked in there at least forced me to analyse where I was heading and it made me realise I did have some control over my destiny. In the end I got out fairly swiftly, a matter of a few days in all, by convincing the psychiatrists that I did not fulfil the criteria for involuntary incarceration.

Once out of Larundel I took things into my own hands and started to get myself under control. It took some time, and most of that year is lost to memory. I know that I owe a lot to Denise and Sue's support and patience. I lived with them for three or four months in 1988. Because I had dropped out of medical school I did not have any work to keep me occupied. I volunteered for part-time work with the Salvation Army to force myself to get back into interacting with people and to do something useful with all my spare time.

I found myself at a cross-roads in my life; I could go one of two ways. I could continue to wallow in my misery and self-pity and either succeed in killing myself or end up back in Larundel. Or, instead, I could take my life into my own hands and forge a path for myself. Finally I knew I was in a position where I had to take responsibility for myself. No longer did I need to be a victim.

I realised that previously Anne had always decided what should happen to me and had made my life hell for eighteen years. But now, finally, *I*, and no one else – no guru, no curse, no predetermined karmic laws – had control over my future, and only I could decide if I wanted to perpetuate that hell in my life, or put it behind me and make it work *for* me, not against me. I applied to re-enter medical school in 1989, determined that I would become a doctor and make my background serve some useful purpose.

It took a couple of years, years spent pretending that I was coping and soldiering on despite being very depressed and miserable, but eventually I began to adapt and actually start to enjoy life. I hadn't realised that I was so depressed: I thought that my unhappiness was a normal state for me. Four years later, in 1992, I suddenly realised that I was no longer unhappy, and that I was beginning to enjoy what I was doing and learning.

After the few months spent with Denise and Sue I moved back into St John's, even though I was over 18 by this time. We kids stayed at St John's for the better part of three years. We moved from the base at Canterbury to a community house in Camberwell. People came and went. Some of my brothers and sisters tried to resettle with their new-found families, but that never worked. A few moved out to a smaller unit towards the end of the three years.

I kept up my friendship with Marie Mohr. I'd known her about a year by this time and I'd go around a couple of nights a week for dinner and end up staying the night. Eventually, in late 1988, she asked if I would like to move in and so I did. I lived with Marie and her husband, Michael, for about twelve months.

They were wonderful to me. They accepted me into their family and taught me a lot about how to be normal and how to enjoy life. I was coping well with university but still often suffered from nightmares and was apprehensive about meeting strangers. I changed a lot in the twelve months that I lived with Marie and Mick and their two crazy animals. It took time and understanding to leave the past behind and I needed some individual care, which a few very special people gave, despite having their motives questioned by almost everyone.

To some extent I am now ambivalent about Anne. I think she's more sick than evil. Seeing her on television being led away in handcuffs, when the task force extradited her from the United States, I felt more pity than anger. Despite everything I don't want to see her suffer. There's no real reason to see her suffer. Revenge isn't a motivating factor in my life. You can't live your life like that, hoping to see people punished for their actions. To a degree her actions are now largely irrelevant to me. I suppose what I am saying is that I have forgiven Anne.

In the early days after leaving the cult, when the kids were having a lot of problems, I used to become very angry with Anne. Sometimes the children felt so lonely and isolated and they couldn't understand the outside world. The only life we'd known was filled with abuse. Thus it is that I only ever feel angry with Anne now when I look around at the other kids and see that they are having problems. I get angry that she won't tell Cassandra who she is: that she still insists that Cassandra is her natural daughter. I find it unforgivable that she could withhold someone's identity. I know how much harder it would have been for me if I hadn't discovered who I was.

I will continue to denounce Anne and protest against what she has done, both to us children and to many others in the cult that she still runs. Even though I forgive her for what she did, I will never cease to denounce it as wrong, and I will continue to try to expose her so that hopefully she will not be able to get away with hurting others in the future. I feel a deep sense of outrage at what she has done to people in the name of spirituality and religion. Anne uses religion for monetary gain and for personal satisfaction. She seems to take delight in causing suffering to others. Destroying life and liveliness in people is perhaps the true definition of evil.

As I write this I can see that I am not sure what I feel about her now. Although I cannot hate her, and even sometimes wish we could sort things out and be a family again, I don't believe in her any more. My belief in her power and the strength of her preaching has been shattered. I know her for what she is. I know that I do not want her to hate me and I do not hate her. Hate is empty and useless and eats you up. I want to show her I survived despite her, and to prove that I can find happiness and personal fulfilment, that I have a belief in myself. These aspirations are all now coming to fruition in my life and that is far more important than hate or revenge.

It is easy to dwell on 'if only' situations. Sometimes I wish that one day we could all sit around a table together and share a cup of tea and put all the negative emotions behind us. Perhaps she still has a little power over me. Secretly, maybe I still love her. I don't know. If she walked into my life now and said, 'I love you, Sarah, and I want you to come back and be part of The Family', I wouldn't do it. But I would have a hard time withstanding her. I'd try to I suppose, but she looms so large in my life. The mother I never had, the mother I craved. She was all there was. Today the prospect of seeing her sent to prison does not do anything for me except make me feel sad: sad for her as well as for me and for all the others. Imprisonment would solve nothing. It certainly wouldn't make what we suffered as children go away.

I see an old woman now when I look at her. I saw her on television after the Federal Bureau of Investigation had arrested her in the United States. She'd been in the bath when they burst into the house and she hadn't had time to fix herself up. She just looked like a pathetic, scared old woman. Maybe the fact that I recognise her as that means that her power over me is lessening. I don't know.

What is the legacy of being the children of Anne Hamilton-Byrne, of being part of The Family? Why was it so hard for us to adapt to the outside world, and why is there that gulf of pain within all of us that will never quite recede? The physical abuse is part of the answer, but the psychological and spiritual ramifications continue also. Self-loathing, feelings of worthlessness and shame, and irrational guilt were our legacy. We were children who lived in a world of deception, lies and inconsistencies. We were children who had been hurt repeatedly and punished for crimes we often hadn't known we'd committed. We were led to believe that we were inherently unworthy – a conviction hard to annul. Feelings of fear and mistrust, and an automatic assumption that others are going to attempt to hurt and betray us, are other legacies of our past. I think there also may be an inability to love, although some of us are starting to overcome this. A sense of powerlessness, too – an assumption that bad things will happen no matter what you do to avoid them, and there is little you can do to change that fact – is a pervading aspect of our childhood that is hard to shake off. There is also a feeling of not belonging to the outside world, a sense that it is too difficult to cope out here.

It is not easy to convey my life to people. I get angry when strangers who know something of my story say things like, 'It can't have been all that bad: look at you now'. What do such people want of us? Do they want to be able to see the scars? Do they want us to be failures? Why would it make more sense if I were a failure? The fact that my childhood has not ruined me is no reflection on the degree of difficulty we have all experienced in coping with our lives. Do people think we must be lying about our childhood, simply because on the surface we appear to be coping? Do they think that I am making it all up?

Often I find myself avoiding saying anything about my past when people ask, especially if they ask silly questions. It's easier that way. Most of the other kids have similar reactions, so in the end there are only a few people we trust, who have been there from the beginning and to whom we don't have to explain the whole thing, and we don't bother with the rest. Where do you begin with strangers?

Others, particularly now that I am doing well, see my name and assume that I am still part of the cult. So I'm fighting my past on two fronts. There are people who are saying that I am not enough of a failure, and there are those who think I must be still active within the cult. All because I am succeeding in life rather than playing the victim. You can't win. Perhaps one day I will change my name. The time will come I think.

Because my past was so strange, it is almost surreal to me now. I find myself sometimes trying hard to work out what reality is and who I am. Because of that and because of the constant doses of tranquillisers we were fed maybe I haven't remembered every detail. Yet I have told the truth as best I can. I know Anne Hamilton-Byrne and her followers will deny it all. They will say I'm lying or I'm mad. I can't worry about that. I must simply tell the truth as I know it.

Even now, many years on, scenes from those days sometimes intrude in my dreams and I wake up at night in a fright thinking I am still at Uptop. Sometimes while working in the children's wards at the hospital, I hear a child screaming and my mind flashes back to Uptop and I get filled with irrational anxiety. I have to make an effort to calm myself and say 'It's all right now, it's over. It is only a dream'. It takes a very long time to put that past behind you, and to totally forget what happened; I think bits of it will occasionally haunt my dreams and echo in my life forever, despite how well I appear to adapt to life in the outside world.

Eventually my brothers and sisters decided to go their separate ways. Living together, particularly in the St John's environment, was not working. Most of us were ready to find our own path, and in some ways the group dynamics were holding back individual maturity and growth. I understand this now, although at the time I fought for us to stay together, desperately wanting to preserve a family that was perhaps always a fantasy. I do believe, however, that it was best for us that we stayed together during those first one or two years, because at that time we needed each other most. Also, I do not believe we would have been given as much support by the State had we split up earlier. Together we were a political force, and the telling of our story over and over again on television could guarantee the politicians' support for new inquiries or changes to legislation that meant adoption searches became swifter.

We live apart now, although we see each other frequently. We get together for birthdays, holidays and special events and drop round to each other's houses for visits often. Every year on 14 August, the day of that fateful police raid on Uptop, we celebrate our Freedom Day. We try to keep in touch with and support each other as best we can. We care about each other and worry about each other like the members of a normal family. We will always love each other despite everything. We consider ourselves brothers and sisters because we shared a childhood together. Our experience has meant that only we can really understand each other. Only we know the full story, the things that cannot be told or explained in an account such as this.

There are many inadequacies of communication between us, many old resentments and guilts, as there are in every family. But only we will ever know and understand the need and pain that exists in each one of us, which is the legacy of our upbringing. And maybe only we can help each other in the healing of that hurt.

As I mentioned before, a police task force called Operation Forest was set up after one of the many media blitzes on our case, about a year and a half after the raid. Its task was specifically to investigate The Family. Several court cases resulted during those early years, usually just before exams or at other awkward times for me. Marie and I both received death threats after one particular media interview, and the police arrested and charged the cult member who threatened us. He ended up pleading guilty to a lesser charge of threats to cause actual bodily harm and got a very light penalty, a suspended gaol sentence. That didn't make trying to get to sleep at night any easier. The cult also tried to sue Channel Nine for Marie's coverage of our story, but backed out before the case got to court when they saw the evidence against them that would be brought to public notice.

But there was to be no justice for what happened to us. Most of the abuse was subject to statutory limitation, which meant that charges could not be laid because a certain period of time had elapsed since the abuses had taken place. The only offences the police ended up charging Anne and her cronies with were connected with frauds involved in securing our false birth certificates and passports. I will never understand just why it all ended this way; maybe I am naive about the system and don't know how things work, but it looks to me like the whole thing was handled badly from beginning to end.

Let me be in a hurry to add that I certainly do not blame the individual police officers concerned for what happened in the inquiry. Although the justice system let us down, I have nothing but praise for the police who were involved in our case. They were caring and diligent and worked long and hard at an incredibly complex case. Several of them gave us much-needed support and assistance on a personal level as well. The strain of working on such a bizarre and draining case took its toll at times on all the police involved.

It took a long period for some of us to accept that there was never going to be any form of retribution for all the years of abuse. But to get on with life, one has to accept that things are not always fair. I have chosen the path of not wasting energy on feelings of bitterness at the system or hatred towards Anne for what she and her minions have done to me. I prefer to forgive and forget. I know the greatest way I can be compensated for and triumph over my childhood is to succeed in what I am doing, to live life fully and to learn what it is to be happy.

If I can do that, I will have won and the cult will have lost. If I can achieve happiness, I will have gained far more for myself than any court case or retribution could have given me. For I will have transcended the legacy of being a child of The Family. I will have transcended the legacy of being a Hamilton-Byrne.

At the end of 1993, during the long summer break, I went to work for the American Refugee Committee on the Thai–Burma border, as part of my medical student elective. I worked with a wonderful group of people, which included an American nurse, a Dutch nursing teacher, a Thai translator and lab technician and a Karen driver (the Karens are one of the indigenous Burmese tribes and constituted the majority of the refugees with whom we were working). We had few people and lots of camps to cover, so for some periods I was left alone to take full medical responsibility.

I was in the heart of the jungle in a camp of 1500 war traumatised and starved Karen refugees in the midst of a malaria epidemic. My referral base, a small border hospital, was an eight-hour drive away, so I could only refer if I thought the patient was going to die unless surgery was performed or if he or she needed more drugs than I had to work with. On the other hand, keeping someone alive in the back of a truck on a night ride through that jungle was not an easy or a pleasant task, as I found out pretty soon.

I saw a lot of what medicine is about while I was on that elective, and experienced a lot of highs and lows. I had the magnificent experience of being able to initiate an intervention – simple drugs and intravenous fluids – that saved the lives of many children dying of malaria. I saw a lot of conditions that I could often do very little about, but there were also times when I could do something or teach someone something that would be very significant – things like building latrines or teaching the carers to wash their hands after being with a sick person, which would mean that many people would not have to die from dysentery and diarrhoea. Sometimes very basic health information and simple drugs could make a hell of a difference to those people's lives. Somehow I felt at last useful in life, as if I was making a significant contribution to these wonderful people. I also experienced the agony of watching patients of mine die, and of being powerless to prevent the pain of the mothers who lost their newborns because they were too small and because of the appalling conditions into which they were born. The experience taught me a lot about why I want to be a doctor.

Confidence as a medical student is easy to exhibit in the big Australian teaching hospitals where you know you don't have people's lives in you hands, and there are laboratories and many people more expert than you to back up your diagnosis and decisions about how to treat the ill person. Up there in the camps my experiences were humbling and frightening at times and it brought home to me the reality of medicine.

Medicine is about pain and suffering and people sometimes dying no matter what you do. It's about blood and sweat – some of it your own – and about hopelessness and tears and feeling like giving up occasionally. But it's also about smiles and gratitude and love and finding peace and courage and wisdom from other people, no matter what language they speak.

Being in the camps taught me about myself. It helped me on the journey to finding out who I am. Sometimes all you could be was a human being.

I'll tell you the story of a little girl – it's another of those stories where little kids' lives don't seem to mean much in the scheme of things. We'd driven to a neighbouring camp one day to check it over. We'd taken a carload of kids just for the ride because they loved to get out of their own camp. As we were leaving, someone ran up to tell us about a little 4-year-old girl who was comatose. Her family had walked for seven days to reach our camp because they had heard that a white doctor was there who could treat malaria, and two of the family's children had died on the walk. This little girl was on the verge of dying, too.

I tried to get an intravenous line into her arm to give her the drugs and fluids that she needed, but I was unable to get it in. I was trying so hard to treat her and everyone in that camp was watching, but I was having no success and I felt like the world's biggest loser. I eventually gave her all the drugs intramuscularly and gave her fluids via a tube into her stomach, but this was far from satisfactory. I decided we had to evacuate her to the referral hospital if she was to survive.

I confess I cried sitting with that dying little girl on the long night drive through the jungle. I cried for her because she had never had a chance and I cried also for myself because I felt so helpless to save her. I felt very alone sitting in the dark with my fingers on her feeble pulse. This little girl came to symbolise for me all the children the world does not care about.

My little girl survived the journey and we finally got her to the referral hospital. She did have cerebral malaria and she was still in a coma five days later when I left. Somehow I don't think she ever woke. But she means a lot to me, that little girl, 4 years old and never given a chance. I know that part of my life will be dedicated to helping little kids like her and I will go back there one day. Those people, and their wonderful spirit, will live in my heart for a long time.

In the summer of 1994 I again went overseas, this time to work in the putrid and overcrowded slums of Calcutta with Calcutta Rescue. I also spent some time with the Ramakrishna Mission, doing seva at a big religious meeting and working with their mobile medical unit in remote villages outside Calcutta. At the Ramakrishna Mission I learnt how to practise medicine in a way that brings great personal joy. Their motto was 'Service to God through Service to Man', and they looked upon each patient as a manifestation of God. Thus for the doctors and nurses involved it became a great privilege to practise medicine, and help people – an attitude far removed from, and much more uplifting than the spirit of 'charity' that pervades many voluntary organisations. Like my work in Thailand, this experience helped me to realise the direction in which I wanted my life to go and reinforced my reasons for practising medicine.

Through medicine, and through making my childhood work for me by enhancing my empathy and compassion for others, I feel that I can make a contribution with my life. I can truly 'serve God through Service to Man'. In the life of a person such as myself, who has had a period of trauma or suffering, meaning comes not necessarily from a renunciation or overcoming of the traumatic experience, but from an acknowledgement that it serves as a unique part of one's life story. My childhood is something that will always be carried with me, but which, if carried well, can be a source of strength and not of despair. My degree in medicine grants me what I believe is an awesome privilege: that of learning about people and playing a part in their lives, of interacting with others in all sorts of settings on an intensely intimate and productive level. I want to make something wonderful out of my life: I am determined that it will be a productive and positive experience from now on. I do not want to waste this future that I have carved out for myself after such a difficult beginning. Medicine offers for me a wonderful tool to do what I can for others, to make a small difference in some lives. It also offers me a passport to exploring and experiencing life: the ultimate and most exciting adventure.